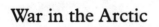

War in the Arctic

WAR IN THE ARCTIC

by

OLAV FARNES

Translated by Christopher Normann

DARF PUBLISHERS

LONDON

Published 1991
By Darf Publishers Ltd

British Library Cataloguing in Publication Data
Farnes, Olav
  War in the Arctic.
  1. Norway. Doctors. World War 2
  I. Title   II. [Lege pamange fronter]. *English*
  940.5475481092

  ISBN 1-85077-220-7

Printed by BPCC Wheatons Ltd, Exeter, Devon
Jacket design by Sue Sharples

This Book is dedicated to Valerie

Introduction

My aim in writing this book has been to give some idea of the work of the medical corps in various theatres of war, based on my own experience as a medical officer in highly varying conditions. Moreover, the war in Svalbard (Spitsbergen) has not previously been described by anyone who took part in it, and I therefore felt obliged to do so, describing it in somewhat greater detail, as it figured prominently in my service outside Norway. This was a special kind of war, with both sides striving for mastery of an area from which vital meteorological information could be relayed, and where a great many tense situations, not generally recorded in the annals of World War Two, were played out. However, the war in Svalbard was only a part of the war in the Arctic, and one has to turn to other areas as well to give a more complete picture.

In the autumn of 1944 I was attached to the British medical service, RAMC, and went to Holland and took part in the invasion of Walcheren; and in 1945 to Belgium where I worked at a British base hospital in Brussels.

Inevitably I have included in my account details of various campaigns and operations that provided the background for the activities of the medical corps.

Thanks to good co-operation between the Norwegian and British services, there were few differences between our medical corps and the way these functioned, neither at the front nor in the rear areas. Serving in war hospitals gave me a great deal of valuable medical experience.

Finally, I describe an episode which all too tragically reveals that, for some unfortunate people, peace, when it came, provided no liberation but the opposite.

The original book was published in Norway in 1947: in this English version I have included a good deal more about the war in the Arctic, more historical facts are added and corrections have been made.

Preface

to the Norwegian edition

Not much has been written about the activities of the medical service in the Norwegian forces during the last war, and this is especially true of its exploits outside the realm.

In this book Dr Olav Farnes presents valuable and interesting information on the Norwegian medical corps serving with Norwegian and Allied formations during the war.

It is no mere coincidence that the orthopaedic surgeon Olav Farnes, one of the relatively few Norwegian medical officers to have served in several theatres of war, should have been the author of this book.

He qualified as a doctor in 1934, and had embarked on his training in surgery when the Finnish winter war broke out in 1939. He soon volunteered, and served in a military hospital. Returning to Norway when the Germans invaded his country, Farnes took part in the fighting in the south of Norway, and when this came to an end, made his way to North Norway, where the Germans were still meeting stubborn resistance.

In 1941 he obtained a post in Bergen as a cover to enable him to make contact with the underground organisation involved in helping Norwegians to escape to Britain. This he succeeded in doing, and eventually reached The Shetlands after a hazardous crossing.

On joining the Norwegian forces in the U.K. Dr Farnes occupied several medical posts in England, Scotland and Iceland.

In 1943 he was asked to join a highly perilous Norwegian expedition to Svalbard (Spitsbergen) earmarked for a special and difficult operation in the Arctic, as yet never described by any of the participants.

On his return to Britain he was attached to the Royal Army Medical Corps, assisting in the run-up to the invasion, and joining a field ambulance during the Walcheren Campaign.

When war ended he was working at a base hospital in Brussels, and from there was ordered back to Norway, concluding his military service with a voyage to Murmansk in a ship carrying Russian prisioners of war who were repatriated.

Olav Farnes has written a thrilling account of his many and varied activities, a book crammed with useful information and of absorbing interest.

CARL Fr. TIDEMANN
Major-General, Director of the
Medical Services in the Norwegian Armed Forces

Contents

At a war Hospital in Finland

Oslo's East Station on a bitterly cold evening in mid-January 1940. A number of doctors who have volunteered to serve at Finnish hospitals are waiting to board their train. Finland has been invaded by Soviet Russia, and is fighting desperately against vastly superior numerical odds.

World War Two had started with Germany's invasion of Poland on September the First, 1939. Sixteen days later, Soviet Russia moved in for her share of the booty, after concluding an agreement with Germany on 23rd August to divide Poland between them. As an added precaution, Russia was anxious to turn Finland into a buffer state between herself and the West, and with this as her aim, she had launched her attack on 30th November, 1939.

In Norway and other western countries various forms of aid for the Finns were organised. From as far afield as America volunteers came to fight shoulder to shoulder with the Finns. The Red Cross despatched field ambulances, while the organisation Norsk Folkehjelp (Norwegian People's Aid) arranged for Norwegian doctors to be sent to Finnish hospitals.

I had managed to obtain leave from my work in the surgical department of Aker Hospital. Now that a state of war existed between Germany and the western powers, experience in wartime surgery might well prove useful. Besides the vast majority of Norwegians were anxious to help the Finns in their unequal struggle.

By next morning we were in Stockholm, and in the course of the morning we boarded a ship bound for Aabo—or Turku in Finnish—on the southwest coast of Finland.

On a crowded train to Jyväskyla we had our first contact with a people at war. There was a spirit of optimism in the air, and even if some of those we met were apprehensive about the outcome of the war, they managed to conceal this. Our arrival was obviously much appreciated: it provided tangible proof that the Finns were not alone.

Jyväskyla is a medium-sized town—by local standards—in the interior of the country. Our arrival coincided with an air raid warning. A Russian plane had been sighted, and we were ordered down into the air-raid shelter where we remained until the all clear sounded. A short rail journey landed us in Änekoski, a village whose only industry consisted of a large paper factory. Here we were billeted in the plant manager's house, a rambling old building. Our hosts proved charming and hospitable.

The hospital, situated some distance away, had been set up in a large and comparatively modern school building. It contained a surgical and medical department, as well as an x-ray unit. Otherwise we had a staff of specialists who travelled round to the various field hospitals. Neurosurgery proved to be our main concern, as there were a great many head injuries. Our particular scene of activity was a so-called base hospital. Many of our patients had already received treatment at a field hospital, where acute cases and the more urgent operations were dealt with. We had a great many shell cases, resulting in large, septic wounds and fractured bones. Bullet wounds were smaller and cleaner. This was, of course, before the days of penicillin, so we used sulpha drugs to overcome infection. Wounds were cleaned, injured tissue, foreign bodies and shell-splinters removed. Fractures were either placed in traction or in a plaster cast, or operated on.

The medical department was in the hands of a doctor from Helsinki, who was also in supreme command of the hospital. As practically all our patients and the staff spoke nothing but Finnish, some of the nurses had to act as interpreters. Our daily fare was simple, but there was no severe rationing, although there was a shortage of a number of things. One day a crate of oranges arrived from Oslo, sent by some friends of ours for distribution among our patients, who were highly appreciative of this gesture.

Outside the temperature often sank to minus 40 degrees Celsius, but the air was dry, and the Finnish fur cap proved indispensable. When the temperature rose to minus 25, after a really cold spell, the air felt positively balmy in the sun. In our spare time we enjoyed some fine skiing.

The casualty lists would occasionally contain the names of local inhabitants, and now and again communal funeral services were held in the village. Optimism, however, remained high, encouraged by reports of successful counter-offensives. The Finnish armed forces were under the competent leadership of Field Marshal Gustav Mannerheim, universally considered the person best qualified to conduct Finland's defensive war.

The bitterest and most decisive battles were fought in Karelia. Further north exceptionally heavy falls of snow made it difficult for the Russians to advance with their tanks and artillery, while the Finns, despite the enemy's numerical superiority, could drive deep behind the Russian lines with fleet-footed ski patrols, and inflict heavy casualties. This boosted morale, and optimism among troops and civilians alike. Everyone hoped for a favourable outcome, everyone, that is, except the Communists, who were generally regarded with the same contempt as the quislings in Norway after the German invasion of 9th April, 1940. The Finns still remembered the bloody civil war of 1918–1919, with Reds and Whites involved in a bitter conflict. By now Soviet Russia had officially recognised a government-in-exile of Finnish Communists led by Otto Kuusinen, which waited in readiness in the border town of Terijoki.

Despite their courageous resistance the Finns were finally forced to abandon the unequal struggle: their superb fighting spirit proved no match for an enemy vastly superior in numbers and in arms. March 13th was a sad day, with the announcement of the terms of the armistice. Considerable areas were ceded to the Russians, particularly in Karelia and North Finland, comprising the loss of some 35,000 square kilometres of Finland's economically most important area, containing more than 10 per cent of her cultivated land and industry.

The consequences of this peace treaty meant that, as Finland had to hand over the Petsamo area in the extreme north, Norway now shared a common frontier with Soviet Russia. This meant that in 1944 the Russians were able to cross straight into Norway's northernmost county, Finnmark, and assist in driving out the Germans.

As there was plenty to keep us busy at the hospital, we stayed on till 9th April. That morning the radio announced that the Germans had invaded Norway. Our Finnish friends were full of sympathy, we were now in the same boat, two small nations caught up in the conflict between super powers.

Arrangements were made to enable us to leave that very day. As we bade farewell we were presented with various gifts, including a special book containing the signatures of all our patients and the staff.

We took the train to Helsinki, which we reached that evening; the Finnish capital carried the scars of aerial bombardment. Next day we flew to Stockholm, where we learned that Mr Hambro, Speaker of the Norwegian Storting (Parliament), and incidentally, as we were to discover, the only person in authority—apart from King Haakon himself—who kept his head during those dramatic April days, was staying at the Grand Hotel. He told us we should make our way to Østfold, the county adjoining Oslo to the south-east, where fighting was in progress, and report for duty.

The war in Norway

We crossed the border into Norway, and were told to report to the hospital in the town of Askim, where help was urgently needed. Only a few kilometres to the west Norwegian and German troops were heavily engaged at Fossum Bridge.

On our way we met scores of young men hanging around, waiting to join their units. They were unarmed, and had received no clear instructions. Obviously mobilisation plans had gone drastically wrong: while a small force of Norwegian troops was being pushed back by an enemy attacking in superior numbers, hundreds of men, eager to do their bit, were forced to remain idle.

We reached Askim to find that the place was being shelled. Our immediate task was to evacuate the hospital. A provisional field dressing station was being set up at Ørje, but shortly afterwards orders were issued for all personnel and material to cross the border into Sweden, as the battle for Østfold was over, despite heroic resistance. The major encounter took place at Fossum Bridge, where 400 Norwegians faced 2,000 Germans. In clashes at nearby Trögstad and Greaker the odds were equally unfavourable. Quite clearly mobilisation orders had been issued too late, and, to make matters worse, many of the senior officers in the field had fallen down on the job.

The streets of Årjäng in Sweden were crowded with Norwegian soldiers. We were well received at the local hospital, where a field ambulance was organised, under the command of the senior doctor from Askim Hospital.

Soon afterward we moved north to Idre, where a road runs across the border to Drevsjö, just north of Trysil. Fighting was reported around Osen, and already Norwegian refugees were streaming across into neutral Sweden. The local doctor in Drevsjø, who had been a member of the Norwegian Nazi party, had hanged himself in a fit of mental aberration, and I took over his practice for a week.

We were finally forced to evacuate, making our way back to Idre. The

Swedes had organised collections of clothing for refugees, and our field ambulance undertook distribution.

Shortly afterwards I returned to Stockholm, where the presence of Norwegian refugees was already making itself felt. After repeated visits to the Norwegian legation and consulate, we were finally given an opportunity of making our way to North Norway, where the war was still in progress, after the collapse of all armed resistance in the south.

We travelled by train to Haparanda in the extreme north of Sweden, close to the border with Finland, and proceeded on a Finnish train to the terminal station at Rovaniemi in Finnish Lapland, on the Arctic Circle. Our journey continued by bus, through a bleak landscape, past mighty Lake Inari, finally crossing the border into Norway, and on to the town of Kirkenes. From there a local steamer would take us as far south as Honningsvaag, but not further, as German bombers posed a constant threat. However, we persuaded the owner of a motorboat to take us down to Tromsø, which was now functioning as Norway's capital, with the King and the government in residence. The town was the scene of frantic activity, its streets thronged with men in uniform or wearing a wide range of sporting clothes.

I was ordered to report to a medical depot at Storsteinnes at the head of the Bals Fjord, and set off with one of the local doctors, who was on his way there to visit a patient. We crossed over by ferry, and then drove along a dirt road with melting ground frost that had clearly not been designed for heavy wheeled traffic. Finally we reached a large medical depot, where a number of doctors were waiting to be sent to the Narvik front, where General Carl Gustav Fleischer and his troops had done so much to rehabilitate Norway's tarnished military reputation, driving the Germans all the way to the Swedish frontier. We medicos were clearly not required, as no one called for our services.

Despite the victories on the Narvik front, North Norway, too, was finally abandoned. The debacle on the western front in France posed a threat to Britain herself, and all British troops were hastily recalled. The King of Norway and his government left for England in the cruiser "Devonshire" for five years of exile. The liberation of Norway would have to be fought for in foreign lands.

The Devonshire left Tromsö in the evening of 7th June with the King, the Crown Prince and a group of 460, politicians, civil servants and British and Norwegian officers, escorted by two destroyers. Luckily her presence was not detected the following afternoon by the German battlecruisers "Scharnhorst" and "Gneisenau" as she passed near the area where these ships at that time were engaged in a battle with the British aircraft carrier "Glorious" and the two destroyers "Ardent" and "Acasta". All three ships were sunk after a short engagement, with the loss of 1,500 lives, a disaster which provoked a debate in the House of Commons, in which gross negligence was alleged.

The day before, the crew of the carrier had been hard at work, as aircrafts from Bardufoss and Narvik landed on the flight-deck for the return voyage to the U.K. All hands were now relaxing as the ship steamed back to Scapa Flow in fine weather and a calm sea. At about 4 p.m. two large ships were sighted on the horizon. As these failed to identify themselves when challenged, a radio signal was sent out reporting the presence of enemy ships, but this was not correctly interpreted on board the Devonshire, which was not far off but was maintaining radio silence, owing to the presence of King Haakon. On the Courageous Swordfish torpedo-bombers were quickly prepared for take-off, a precaution that had been neglected. Suddenly plumes of water reared up around the ship, followed by the sound of gunfire. The next salvo went through the flight-deck, bursting in the hangar below, destroying the aircrafts and exploding the ammunition. Another salvo hit a gun turrent and the bridge killing the captain and nearly everybody inside. The ship was soon ablaze, but continued at full speed to the south-east making a maximum speed of 27 knots, but the Germans were gaining on them from the northwest at 29 knots. When the engine-room was hit the Germans closed in and the battle lasted for some time with the destroyers courageously attacking the larger ships, getting in several hits with gunfire and torpedoes before they all three were sunk. Many went down with the ships and many who had scrambled onto the floats perished from exposure, as it took a couple of days before help arrived.

Shortly afterwards normal coastal steamer services were resumed, and we made our way south to the ancient city of Trondheim. Germans were waiting on the quay when we landed, but we were spared any kind of systematic control, and shortly afterwards boarded a train for Oslo.

In Oslo the Germans had requisitioned Aker Hospital and turned it into their main hospital, while "my" original Aker Hospital had found temporary accommodation in Berg School in the western suburb of Sogn Garden Village, where I resumed my work.

Across the North Sea to Britain

I'm standing on a quay at the head of a fjord somewhere on the west coast of Norway. In a crowd of some twenty or so men, each of us casting occasional covert glances at the others, as the motorboat that landed us chugs off back down the fjord.

After a while one or two of my fellow passengers engage in a whispered conversation, and I realise that they are old acquaintances.

After a few minutes a man strolls down to the quay, eyeing us quizzically; not surprising, as we must have presented an unusual sight, an assorted bunch of men in sporting clothes of various kinds, and carrying rucksacks, gathered together on a quay in West Norway. He glances out to sea, on the lookout for a German patrol boat, whose crew would obviously have their worst suspicions confirmed.

He exchanges a few words with those nearest him, and I realise that this is our contact.

We follow him up to a large lake, where a couple of rowing boats are drawn up on the shore. We row across to the other side, where we are faced with a stiff climb. The leaders set off at a brisk pace, and I have a hard time of it keeping up. I haven't taken much exercise recently; besides I'm carrying a heavy rucksack packed with medical supplies. After a while we reach flatter ground, and arrive at a number of huts, where we put up.

During the summer of 1941 I had worked as a locum in the Bergen emergency clinic after completing my time at Aker. I had no immediate prospects, and wanted to continue where I had left off after my Finnish interlude. With this in mind I tried to contact someone who could assist me in getting across to Britain. But as a stranger in Bergen I found this difficult: no-one knew much about me.

However, in time I got to know someone who was said to be engaged in anti-German intelligence work, and apparently ran a suitable "travel agency". He was a student of psychology, and was shrewd enough to have moved in to the Bristol Hotel, which swarmed with Gestapo officers. I was shown a radio transmitter he had concealed on the premises, and which the Germans never discovered. But he was not in a position to organise any transport for me.

The emergency clinic was housed in the same building as the police station, and we co-operated closely with the police. One day I gave a hint of my plans to Kjell Krüger, the doctor for whom I was standing in, and this probably set in train what subsequently happened.

When I had done my spell as a locum I left Bergen to visit relatives living by the Hardanger Fjord. One day I received an anonymous postcard, asking me to return to Bergen and ring a particular phone number. Travelling by motorboat and bus I reached Bergen the same day, where I received the following instructions: "Make your way to the Strand Quay early the day after tomorrow. Board the local steamer for Knarvik. Wear hiking clothes and carry a rucksack. When you reach Knarvik, follow the other passengers who are similarly attired."

I had just been told that I had been appointed to the post of assistant doctor in the surgical department of Aker Hospital. I was to have taken up my new post on September the First. I was tempted to do so, but I now had an opportunity of getting to the west. Besides, I felt I would be more useful working with Norwegian military units which were to be established in the U.K. For this reason I cabled the Senior Doctor and turned down the offer. I was anxious to know what the consequences would be. The doctor involved was not particularly noted for his patriotic sentiments, and, as I later discovered, the police were soon making enquiries about me.

I turned up at the Strand Quay as instructed, and boarded the boat which was crammed with passengers. Apart from German troops I noticed a number of men carrying rucksacks scattered among the other travellers.

When we got to our destination I had no difficulty in finding the right bus. All I had to do was to follow the other rucksacks. We drove to the northern shore of the Lindaas peninsula, and got off at Sevraasvaag, where we boarded a motorboat which operated a scheduled run to Austfjord, an arm of the Fens Fjord. This boat carried us across to Kvingo, where we disembarked at the quay I have already referred to. The lake we crossed was Kvingevann.

To the north of the huts where we spent the night a chain of hills ran all the way to the Sogne Fjord.

It was in this terrain that the "Bjørn West" resistance group operated during the last winter of the war. As late as May 1945 the Germans launched a major offensive against these men, deploying substantial forces, and attacking on several fronts, suffering about 100 dead. Eight Norwegians were killed.

Our contact and my fellow-passengers eyed me with considerable suspicion, as I was a stranger. One of the dangers involved in these escapes to freedom is the risk of informers. Everyone knows of parties who have been betrayed in this way, and of men who have been executed by the Germans. There is every reason therefore to exercise caution where strangers are concerned. One never knows who or what the next man may be.

Later I was told that there had been talk of dropping me overboard as we rowed across the lake. I don't know how serious this threat was, but it was a good story when it was subsequently passed on to me.

Next day we were joined by a number of newcomers, including two Bergen police constables, who knew me and were prepared to vouch for me.

In the evening of 31st August we scrambled down the steep hillside. It was dark, and my heavy rucksack was an extra hazard. We all got down in one piece, and rowed back across the lake. Down at the quay where we had landed a few days earlier the same motorboat on which we have arrived was moored. Our voyage across the North Sea was about to begin.

Our leader was Monrad Kvinge. He had spent a long time planning this trip, laying in stores of provisions and oil. But he had no suitable boat. One of his neighbours had one of about the right size, and Kvinge had asked him what he would do if his boat were stolen. Well, was the answer, there would not be much one could do except to report the theft.

"But in that case, you'd have to kick up a hell of a fuss, otherwise maybe you might be suspected of all sorts of things", was Kvinge's advice. This in due course was precisely what the man did, and he suffered no particular harassment after his boat had been well and properly stolen. What's more, it was returned to him after the war.

Kvinge had worked for several years as a coastal pilot, and was familiar with the waters of western Norway: and—more important still—he knew all about the German patrol system up and down the coast, and the position of the mine fields.

Our boat was the "Leda". There were 27 of us on board all told; three of them were women, including Kvinge's wife.

Most of us were promptly ordered below deck. Our aim was to get as far out to sea as possible before daybreak, before we were reported missing and a search set on foot. We set off with dimmed lights. Mist reduced visibility. Suddenly we caught sight of a boat looming through the mist and bearing down on us. A German patrol launch? All hands were ordered below, leaving the skipper in his wheelhouse alone on deck. The tension is electric. Yes, it is a German patrol boat, and we wonder . . . is this journey's end? No, glory be! The strange craft proceeds on her way without challenging us! We head for the open sea and freedom, leaving Mongstad to port, into the teeth of a south-east gale and a choppy sea, the start of our nightmare.

Everyone is seasick, including the skipper. Even hardened seadogs are forced to make their oblation to the fishes, unaccustomed as they are to the choppy motion of a small craft. Below deck the stench is intolerable. Moving across the cabin floor, slippery with vomit, is a hazardous undertaking, but once in a while I have to go below and dole out what little I have in the way of anti-seasick medicine; only suppositories would do. My stomach registers a protest, and I am forced to go back on deck, where I am immediately drenched with spray. As I cling to the rail the piercing wind chills me to the marrow.

I make my way below again. I must have a little rest and warmth. My stomach heaves. The companion-way is forrard; the hatch has been battened down, and all movable gear securely lashed fast. We are all in a miserable state, and to add to our misery the engine gives up the ghost next day, in the middle of the North Sea. Our boat no longer answers to her helm, and she rolls more viciously than ever. Standing aft I cling to the rail, while our engineer works like a Trojan down in the engine-room to get her going. Now and again a pale face appears above the entrance to the engine-room, sending a thin stream of spew across the deck, before disappearing down below.

One and all we dread the thought of German planes, but no one voices these fears. We're not even half-way across. If only the engine would start! She splutters, then stops . . . once again she comes to life, picks up, and finally settles down to an even throb. We all breathe a sigh of relief.

All that day the bad weather persists. To some extent we get used to feeling seasick, while the strange feeling that comes with seasickness, a complete indifference to what might happen, grows. Next day the sea is calmer. A plane approaches from the east. We stand aghast. But as it continues on its way to the west we realise with relief that it's British.

The following morning we start to look for a landfall. We should be getting there by now. An RAF plane flies over, waggling its wings in a gesture of welcome. We can't have far to go now. We don't quite trust our compass. It's mounting broke as we rolled and pitched. The skipper secured it with string, and checked with the Pole Star and the Great Bear, which he caught a glimpse of through a break in the clouds.

When we finally make a landfall we sail through a minefield, nosing our way between horn mines. We arrive at the southernmost point of the Shetlands at Sumburgh Head, and then follow the coast north to Lerwick, escorted by a British vessel. In the harbour a veritable armada of Norwegian fishing smacks and motorboats, all of which have crossed the North Sea, are moored or at anchor. The "Leda" now joins this motley fleet.

Many of these boats were later to play a valiant role in the famous Shetland Bus service, which made such a vital contribution to Norway's resistance movement.

Kvinge's store of provisions consisted, among other things, of a number of tins of canned food, which the Lerwick customs officials studied with a certain measure of suspicion. They were all opened, and—so we were later informed—fed to the local pigs.

Two of our party, Billy Fortun and Ingebrigt Valderhaug, were members of the so-called Stein Group, one of the three resistance cells in Bergen that had been active ever since 1940. As well as gathering intelligence, they assisted Norwegians in getting across to Britain. Valderhaug was a radio operator. Together with Fortun he transmitted messages to England from the so-called "Ladies' House", where they had installed their transmitter. Both of them had already made the trip across the North Sea, and shortly after arrival they were to return to Norway. Fortun and forty persons with him went down with the "Blia" on their way back to Britain in November of the same year. Only a month before Valderhaug and nine others had been arrested and sent to Germany, where, after two years in prison and undergoing severe torture, they were beheaded. All the other members of our party returned to Norway after the war. Kvinge joined the navy, and put his knowledge of Norwegian coastal waters to excellent use.

In Lerwick we were duly registered, and transport was organised to enable us to proceed south. With a few others I set off in an open motorboat. It had a good turn of speed, and we had a fine trip in superb weather and a calm sea—quite a contrast to our North Sea adventure.

The same evening we were billeted in a private house in Buckie, in Scotland, and next day we travelled by train to London via Aberdeen.

The following week we spent at an institution known as the Royal Victoria Patriotic School in the south of London, where persons who had escaped from Nazi-occupied Europe were interrogated and screened. We were thoroughly grilled on conditions in Norway and on our own activities. The whole procedure was conducted in a relaxed manner, but it was obvious that the British authorities were on their guard against German agents.

As soon as I had been cleared I reported to Major Gunnar Johnson, formerly director of Oslo emergency clinic and now head of the Norwegian Medical Corps. His offices were in Norway House, in Cockspur Street, adjoining Trafalgar Square, in the same building as the Norwegian Club, where the King and Government met every week for a conference.

We were lodged in a hotel near King's Cross Station, a practical arrangement, as this was the departure point for trains to Scotland, where the Norwegian forces were stationed. I was given enough time to find my way around, and to procure a khaki uniform and other necessary items of equipment.

London bore the scars of severe aerial bombardment. The City in particular had suffered during the blitz, with large areas a mass of rubble. In the middle of a wilderness of broken masonry and assorted rubbish the huge bulk of St Paul's Cathedral stood proud and practically unscathed. Barrage balloons suspended high above London's parks were a feature of wartime London. These were especially prominent above the great expanse of Hyde Park.

While in London I called on General Fleischer and his wife, who were now living in one of the northern suburbs. He had commanded the 6th Division, stationed in Mosjøen just south of the Arctic Circle when I was there in 1936 as a medical officer of health. During the fighting around Narvik he commanded the Norwegian forces that drove the Germans back all the way to the Swedish border, thus inflicting on Hitler's Wehrmacht their first defeat. Despite this success the campaign in North Norway was abandoned. He was now in command of the Norwegian army in Britain. A few months later he was dismissed from his post, the victim of intrigues contrived by fresh arrivals from Norway. He took this very much to heart, but there was little he could do in the face of people who claimed to represent the Norwegian underground, men who exercised considerable influence in government circles.

Fleischer naturally felt that he had been shabbily treated. He was transferred to a new appointment in Canada, where he ended his life. His widow continued living in London, constantly harassed by cantankerous individuals from Norwegian government offices, eager to lay their hands on any papers the general might have left. Though what they were after is anybody's guess . . . perhaps someone might be compromised?

Iceland

My first posting took me to Iceland, where I was to work as chief medical officer to the Norwegian armed forces stationed there. I took the train to Ayr in West Scotland, where there was an RAF station, and here I remained for two weeks, waiting for a following wind and favourable weather conditions. The problem was that available aircraft had a limited radius of action, and until the right weather dawned there was nothing for it but to wait.

Patience is undoubtedly a virtue, but constantly cocking an eye at the clouds proved in the long run a bit of a bore. An English colonel was in the same predicament as myself. One day we drove to Greenock on the Clyde, having heard that a troop ship would be leaving for Iceland. Great was my surprise when I saw that the ship concerned was the Norwegian America Line's "Bergensfjord", which was embarking troops. We approached the British duty officer, but without success. The ship was overcrowded, and we were forced to return to the RAF station to continue our vigil.

We finally got away in a Hudson bomber, perched on makeshift seats near the tail of the aircraft. We glided down across the coast of Iceland in brilliant sunshine, which gave us a superb bird's-eye view of the Saga Isle, a strange landscape with its mountains, volcanoes and glaciers. The harbour in Reykjavik was crammed with ships, and the airfield bristled with planes.

Iceland had been occupied by units of the Royal Navy as early as May 1940, in the face of a formal protest from the Icelandic government. In the course of the summer, units of the army and the RAF followed, and a base was established at Hvalfjördur north of Reykjavik. The aim of the occupation was to prevent German forces establishing themselves in the island, as well as providing better protection for Allied shipping in the Atlantic against enemy U-boats.

After Britain had concluded the Lease-Lend agreement with the U.S.A. on 11th March, 1941, the Americans assisted in protecting the convoys, and in August of that year the first American air bases were set up in Iceland. In the spring of 1942 the U.S.A. assumed responsibility for the defence of the island, both at sea and on land, releasing British troops who could now be deployed in other theatres of war.

After the Norwegian campaign had been abandoned, an increasing number of fishing smacks and other vessels made their way across the North Sea. Some of these were then armed and commissioned for service in coastal defence, with Norwegian crews and Norwegian naval officers. These were under the command of Captain Ernst Ullring, with the Royal Navy exercising overall control. Ullring had already made a name for himself with his exploits in the destroyer "Sleipner". In the summer of 1940 Ullring arrived in Iceland and was given command of the patrol vessel "Fridtjof Nansen", and made several voyages to East Greenland and the island of Jan Mayen, often in appalling weather. The aim of these forays was to check on the Norwegian meteorological stations in Jan Mayen and in Myggbukta and Torgilsbu in Greenland, and at the same time prevent the Germans establishing stations of their own there.

Jan Mayen, a Norwegian possession ever since it was annexed in 1929, is a volcanic island, covering 370 square kilometres, and situated at approximately 71° Northern latitude and 7° longitude West, a good way east of Greenland and about halfway between Iceland and Svalbard (Spitsbergen). It takes its name from the Dutch explorer who discovered it in 1614. Bleak and inhospitable, for much of the year it is enveloped in fog and surrounded by stormy seas. There is no quay to greet the visitor, and landing on the island is at the best of times a tricky business. Jan Mayen is dominated by a volcanic peak, 2,300 metres high, named Beerenberg, which often looms above the fog, bathed in sunlight, with its crater-like peak, and glaciers draped down its flanks. Very occasionally the mountain growls, spewing out its streams of glowing lava. The last time was in September 1970. It is situated in an area which determines the weather over a considerable distance, owing to the influence of the cold inland ice-cap on Greenland. This spreads cold air, which, coming into contact with the warmer air of the Gulf Stream, produces the fog that is such a prevalent feature of the area.

Already in July 1940 the Germans had dispatched the Norwegian Meteorological Institute's boat "Vaarglimt" to Jan Mayen, with a relief crew of four. Early in September Ullring raided the German station, capturing its personnel and destroying the transmitter as it had been decided to close it down. In November 1940 a message had been intercepted indicating that a German expedition was on its way to Jan Mayen on board the Norwegian sealer "Veslekari". Ullring was ordered to investigate, and immediately set off in the "Fridtjof Nansen", which went aground off Eggøya. The 68 hands on board took to the boats and were picked up by the "Honningsvaag", a former German trawler now a Norwegian coastguard vessel stationed in Iceland. It had originally turned up in Honningsvaag North-Norway hoping to meet some Germans there, but these had not yet arrived, and the boat was promptly seized by the local dentist and handed over to the Norwegian navy.

Units of the Royal Navy patrolling the Denmark Strait between Iceland and Greenland then dispatched a number of ships to intercept the German expedition, whose boat went aground and broke up, her crew being captured and the remains of the station destroyed.

In time it was decided that the needs of the convoys operating in the Atlantic required a meteorological station in Jan Mayen, but it was also realised that it would be necessary to install a garrison in order to defend it. Owing to adverse weather it proved impossible to organise this before the Spring of 1941. Officers and other ranks were drawn from the Norwegian ski company in Iceland. This had been raised by Lieutenant Karl Hjelvik in the autumn of 1940, at the request of the British. It was subsequently expanded with the addition of men from the Norwegian Brigade in Scotland. At first it was stationed outside Reykjavik, but owing to poor snow conditions there, it was transferred to Akureyri on the north coast, where there was in addition a camp up in the mountains. The unit consisted of about one hundred of all ranks, half of whom at a time served on Jan Mayen, where a medical student was posted as the unit M.O.

The ski company, which also was training British and American troops, was disbanded in 1944.

The Jan Mayen station was set up in 1941 in Jøssingdalen, between the North and South Lagoon, making it invisible from the sea. On 15th July, 1942, a JU 88 was shot down and crashed into the mountainside. Three weeks later the station was bombed by a Focke-Wulf 200. After several hits it fell on the rocky wall, killing its crew of four, who were buried with full military honours. In May another four-engine plane had flown over and dropped its bombs. It was hit by anti-aircraft fire, and an explosion was later heard over the coast to the south.

Throughout 1942, in fact, there was considerable activity on the part of German aircraft and U-boats in the air and waters around the island. But time and again fog prevented them from carrying out an attack, while at the same time the anti-aircraft defence improved.

In September 1944 a U-boat set up an automatic met. station, "Walter", in Krossbukta on the north coast, but it was discovered by the Norwegians the following January.

It was important for the Germans to obtain meteorological reports from this area once the Norwegian stations had started encoding their messages, and for this reason they also made use of aircraft.

After the tour of inspection of Jan Mayen in November 1940, when the "Fridtjof Nansen" struck a rock and foundered, Ullring was placed in command of the Norwegian patrol vessels. In June 1941 he was appointed to command all Norwegian forces in Iceland, with the exception of air force units, which were directly subordinate to the RAF.

All in all some half dozen armed Norwegian vessels were employed on patrol duties around Iceland.

In Reykjavik there was a naval base, with offices, a depot and messes.

Ullring was a sociable but somewhat unusual character, with very decided views on various subjects. We were always made welcome in the mess, where Ullring had placed by his seat an empty shell-case from one of "Sleipner's" four guns. This now served as a gong, to be struck when anybody wanted a drink . . . which we certainly did!

However, relations between Ullring and the resident Norwegian Minister were not of the best. The minister and air force personnel, too, were not exactly the best of friends. Not infrequently, as we know, civilian and military authorities tend to tread on one another's toes. For this reason the Norwegian consul proved a useful go-between.

In April 1941 a Norwegian Royal Air Force squadron, from the naval air service, arrived in Reykjavik from the "Little Norway" training camp in Toronto, Canada, replacing an RAF unit at Corbett Camp just south of the Icelandic capital. Wings were established on the north and east coast, at Akureyri and Budareyri respectively. A medical student was attached to each wing, and there was also a unit M.O. in the camp at Reykjavik.

The squadron was equipped with Northrop single-engine seaplanes, armed with machine-guns, bombs and mines. They were employed in protecting Allied convoys in the Atlantic against German aircraft and U-boats, as well as in coastal defence in Iceland. They were frequently in action, on one occasion forcing a U-boat to surface, and escorting it ashore, as well as inflicting damage on numerous German planes and U-boats, though not without suffering substantial losses in men and material.

The camp was not much to boast of, situated in rather marshy ground near the sea, and in rainy weather more like a quagmire, where one moved on duckboards from one Nissen hut to another. These corrugated iron structures, an indispensable feature of every British camp, transportable and easy to mass-produce, were not exactly ideal from a medical officer's point of view.

Prior to my arrival the medical service had been in the hands of Adam Egede-Nissen (no relation of the inventor of the Nissen hut!), and he continued to serve as M.O. to the Norwegian Air Force units. For a while I was also responsible for the Norwegian hospital, as well as having to undertake tours of inspection to the various other establishments.

The hospital had been set up in a large private house which the Norwegian government had purchased. It contained 25 beds, intended for military and civilian personnel. We enjoyed excellent relations with the University hospital in Reykjavik, which was able to deal with more serious cases. During my time in Iceland our patients included a ship's crew that had spent fourteen days on a liferaft in the Atlantic after their vessel had been torpedoed, and were in a state of extreme exhaustion. Thanks to good treatment they made a speedy recovery.

After I had spent a month at the hospital I was able to hand over to a doctor from Canada. He was an Austrian Jew who had settled in Norway before the war. When the Germans invaded, he fled to Canada, where, owing to an administrative error, he was interned in a camp together with a number of Germans, who assaulted him and knocked him unconscious. The hospital staff also included a dentist and his assistant. All nursing staff and other pesonnel were Norwegian.

On one of my tours of inspection to Akureyri I flew in a plane with Hans A. Bugge at the controls. He was O.C. of the Norwegian Squadron, a most likeable person who unfortunately failed to return from a mission later that year.

On this flight we enjoyed splendid weather, and had a superb view of Iceland as we flew over the mountains. The unit M.O. in Akureyri was a highly efficient medical student. We inspected the local camp, as well as the ski company's camp outside the town. Conditions were reasonably good in both places, though somewhat primitive up in the mountain camp.

The climate in Iceland is comparatively mild, particularly on the west coast, which had a great deal of wind and rain. We once experienced a hurricane, with the sea-spray blowing straight in from the west with such force that it was almost impossible to move about out of doors. When the storm abated all west-facing windows were covered with a layer of salt. A great many aircraft were badly damaged, and several ships in the harbour dragged their moorings and went aground.

At the time I was involved in a rather unpleasant case: the Norwegian Minister had got it into his head that a senior-ranking officer was behaving strangely, and needed to be placed under observation. He persuaded the hospital doctor to go along with this. I wrote to London, and submitted the case to the Director of Medical Services, who at this time was Professor Johan Holst. He had the officer recalled to London, where it was decided that there was nothing remarkable about his behaviour, although he did have certain peculiarities. It was realised, however, that his relations with the Minister were somewhat strained, for which reason he was transferred from his appointment in Iceland and given an English posting. For the remainder of his time during the war he served with great distinction, as indeed he had done previously.

I subsequently felt that I had been rather unpleasantly manipulated on the basis of personal incompatibilities which were no concern of mine.

Now and again, as the senior diplomatic representative of his country, the Minister held receptions, where we had an opportunity of meeting Norwegian residents in Reykjavik. These were for the most part businessmen, who had left West Norway, and settled in the town. They were a hospitable lot, always ready to invite us to their homes. Relations between Icelanders and Norwegians were tolerably good. Inevitably there were "incidents": Icelandic youths and Norwegian air force personnel could not always agree on the question of courting the girls. In certain cases these disputes were liable to develop into major street brawls.

There was not much to occupy one's leisure hours. A few enterprising souls hired or bought Icelandic ponies, and rode off inland to enjoy the hot springs or geysers, where it was possible to bathe under the open sky. At that time water conduits were being built to convey hot water from the springs to a hot water plant for the capital, and a large modern swimming bath was already in working order.

After the American presence started to make its impact, access to provisions and other desirable commodities proved easier. There had admittedly been no noticeable rationing as far as the armed forces were concerned, but it was not always easy for the local population to lay their hands on that little bit of something extra. The price of alcoholic beverages on the black market was high, and certain members of the armed forces took advantage of this.

It was always a pleasure to drop in on the air force camp in the evening, when the men were relaxing after completing tiring and often perilous missions. Every guest was always made to feel welcome, but on one occasion their hospitality was poorly rewarded. Stopping off in Iceland on his way from the U.S.A. to London, Professor Leiv Kreyberg was as usual well received in the air force mess. On his arrival in London he drafted a report in which he berated the extravagant standard of living enjoyed by air force personnel, compared with wretched conditions in Norway. They found it difficult to forgive him for this; and considering the dangerous nature of their work, Professor Kreyberg revealed a poor sense of psychology.

Norwegian aircrew were stationed in Iceland until the end of 1942. They had lately been equipped with Catalina twin-engine flying boats, which had a very considerable range and were admirably suited for convoy service.

When the Americans assumed responsibility for all flying duties in Iceland, the Norwegian air force units moved over to Scotland. This was early in 1943. Later they were stationed at the Sullum Voe air base in the Shetlands, from where they carried out convoy service in four-engine Sunderland flying boats with crews of ten.

With the departure of Norwegian personnel from Iceland, the Norwegian hospital was closed down, a task undertaken by my successor Kaare Varvin. The Americans were now in sole charge.

The Norwegian Brigade in Scotland

In March 1942 I was recalled from Iceland and posted as Senior M.O. to the Norwegian Brigade in Scotland. This had been raised in Dumfries in south-west Scotland, and consisted initially for the most part of whaling crews on their way from the South Atlantic whaling grounds who were making their way to the U.K. when Norway was occupied by the Germans. They were now stationed north of Aberdeen, with Brigade H.Q. in Banff, a battalion at Cruden Bay, and other units at Peterhead and Fraserburgh. The Brigade Commander was General Oscar Strugstad, and the Battalion Commander Lieutenant-Colonel Gustav Just. Shortly after my arrival the brigade moved to Cromarty, north of Inverness. H.Q. was set up at Dingwall, and the staff billeted in an old castle, Brahan Castle. The machine-gun company was installed at Strathpeffer further west. Further north we had a coastal battery at Evanton, the battalion at Tain, and still further north the training company in the seaside resort of Dornoch.

Brahan Castle was situated in a spacious park, notable for its wealth of multi-coloured rhododendron bushes. At the end of a long drive the main building was reached; this was a pleasant old stone building fronting a wide courtyard, with a broad avenue of trees leading down to the River Connon, which was well stocked with salmon. A wide staircase ascended to the hall, on the right of which were the premises requisitioned for military use, together with adjacent buildings at the back of the house.

*Brahan Castle was built by Colin Mackenzie after he had been raised to the peerage as the First Earl of Seaforth in 1611. The castle has an interesting history, and was the scene of numerous dramatic events during the many wars and risings of the 17th and 18th centuries. The fifth earl, an ardent supporter of the Stuarts, forfeited both his title and his estates, after the failure of the rising in 1715. His successors were converted to Protestantism, and refrained from taking sides. The 7th

---

*John Prebble: Mutiny.

Earl of Seaforth was restored to his lands and title in 1778, when he raised the Seaforth Highlanders, a regiment recruited from among his tenants and clansmen, with Brahan Castle as its headquarters and training centre. Disciplinary methods used by the officers, and learned from English colleagues who had seen service abroad, were often harsh and, as the spirited Highlanders refused to be cowed, there were frequent mutinies in the Scottish regiments. The Seaforth Highlanders were no exception. The officers were billeted in the castle, where they could admire portraits of Mary Queen of Scots, Darnley and others in the gallery of ancestral portraits, while in the grounds outside redcoats would have provided a splash of colour. Nowadays the many rhododendron bushes have replaced them.

Being on the whole less amenable to discipline Highland regiments were the first to be sent overseas to the colonies. The intention had been to dispatch the Seaforth Highlanders to America to help put down the revolt of the colonists, and this rumour was well received, as so many of the men had relatives who had emigrated to the New World. But on the march to Edinburgh, where they were to embark, they heard rumours that they were bound for India, for service with the East India Company. At Edinburgh Castle several hundred of them mutinied, and refused to march to Leith, where ships awaited them. They complained of their officers, demanded their pay, and refused to be sent to India. After considerable negotiation, in which the earl himself, the "little lord", took part, their demands were met, much against the will of the Commander-in-Chief in London, Lord Amherst.

Although they had won a temporary victory, their subsequent history was to prove tragic. After spending a few years in the Channel Islands the regiment sailed for India. In the course of a voyage lasting little short of a year, several hundred, including the earl himself, died of scurvy before they finally reached Madras. On their arrival in India many were in such an enfeebled state of health that they fell an easy prey to tropical diseases. To add to their misery, contrary to agreement, they were discharged without any means of securing their passage home. Few of them ever saw their beloved Highlands again.

The Earl died without an heir.* But his cousin Major Humbertson, who was also his second-in-command, bought up the Seaforth estate. By

---

*This had been prophesied by the "Brahan Seer", a well known figure in Highland history. All his four sons died, only daughters were left. At Fortrose a monument commemorates the legend of Coinneach Odhar, the "Brahan Seer", who was burnt in tar by order of Lady Seaforth.He had told her of having seen her husband in the arms of another woman in Paris, where he was British envoy, and had prophesied the doom of the family. At Fortrose there is also a protrait gallery of the family, and inside the church-ruins the inscriptions over their graves can still be read.

the time of World War II this belonged to the Mackenzie family. In the 18th. century the castle was "modernised" and spoiled by removing the crenellation. It was pulled down in 1956 after a fire had broken out in the attic. On a recent visit I found cows grazing in a green meadow where the castle had once stood. The magnificent trees in the park were still standing, as proud as ever. On the whole the standard of hygiene was good, though there were certain shortcomings, especially where the much used Nissen huts, already mentioned, were concerned.

Most of the units had their own medical officer, but apart from making rounds of inspection I also had to act as M.O. for some of them. Every unit had a medical corporal to assist the M.O. in his work. At Brigade level medical problems were in essence not different from what might be expected in peacetime, apart from the fact that the whole set-up was now more makeshift. Recruits were examined before a medical board, assigned a category, and posted to the unit for which they were considered most suitable. The unit M.O.'s job was to carry out the necessary inoculations, check sanitary conditions, and deal with any complaints. Stretcher-bearers were to be trained in first aid in the field and transport of wounded on stretchers. In battle conditions these would be brought to an advanced dressing station, ADS where initial medical treatment would be given. If further surgical treatment were required, wounded would be sent to a field hospital by ambulance, or still further in the rear to a base hospital.

In the Brigade we had few cases of serious illness or injury. These could be transported to the Norwegian hospital at Craiglockhart in Edinburgh, which had a surgical and a medical ward. There was also a Norwegian hospital at Newlands near Dumfries, and in addition we had the use of a number of convalescent homes, such as the one at Knockespock to the north-west of Aberdeen.

We had a pretty clean bill of health. With constant training the troops were in good physical shape. Actually one of the few serious cases we had to deal with involved one of the unit medical officers. He was always moving around on his motorbike, and was involved in an accident which resulted in a chest injury and the collapse of one lung. He was speedily transported to Edinburgh. But before long he was back on his motorbike, a tempting form of conveyance on the excellent roads, and one which I personally preferred to being driven in a car.

Flat feet are a common ailment. It doesn't always involve physical pain, and cannot really be classified as an illness. But life in the army, with long and unaccustomed route-marches, is apt to exacerbate the complaint, no matter how physically active one has been in civilian life.

32

For this reason it cannot be right for men with flat feet to be dismissed outright as unfit for combat duties, as was the practice at one time.

This rule was no longer observed: after all, there was a war on. Besides, the increased use of motorised transport made less demand on the feet, and as a result recruits with flat feet were accepted for military service and occasionally for combat duties.

The incidence of flat feet varies from race to race. Among desert people it is of common occurrence, due to the fact that they spend much of their time walking in soft sand. This tends to weaken the arch of the foot, as it does not get a proper "kick-off" with the ball of the foot. A genetic factor may also be involved.

Malingering was less common than it had been in pre-war days. Everyone was more prepared to do his fair share, though occasionally a few would try to "swing the lead", especially before a long route march or strenuous exercise. Very often the M.O. would find himself in a dilemma: on the one hand there was the soldier, who said he was ill; on the other his superior officer, who was convinced he was malingering. No matter what the M.O.'s decision, he was often liable to court unpopularity. But there were few cases of men trying to have themselves declared unfit for service: most of them were animated by a true sense of honour.

The task allotted to the Brigade was to defend its own sector along the north-east coast of Scotland, and for this purpose exercises in the field were held in company with British troops. During one of these exercises the medical services were grossly neglected; I therefore sent a report to the senior medical officer in London calling his attention to this. It was passed on to higher authorities, and finally returned to the Brigade Commander with a reprimand. The latter was not exactly delighted, but this had the desired effect, and from then on our work was more highly appreciated.

The General was a keen salmon fisher, and would set off every day along the river bank with his tackle. The only drawback was that the salmon didn't exactly find his flies to their taste. He just didn't get a bite.

One weekend I made my way to Edinburgh, where I purchased a salmon rod and some flies. On my first visit to the river a twenty-pound salmon took a fancy to the fly I cast. We had an exciting tussle, upstream and down, before I managed to coax the fish onto a sandbank.

There was great hilarity when I turned up with my salmon. The General had fished for days on end with his splendid tackle without luck, and along comes a novice and shows him up! Talk of beginner's luck! Well, he took it nicely, not least after the cook had rigged up a smoke-house of sorts at the back of the house and smoked salmon was served for breakfast. This proved a welcome change from otherwise spartan fare.

As already mentioned, most of the other ranks at first consisted of whaling crews, with the county of Vestfold, south-west of Oslo, strongly represented. Men from the merchant navy swelled the ranks, and after a while, as more people made their way, often by devious routes, to the U.K., we had a more even mix. Many of them were enthusiastic young men keen to see active service as soon as possible. They soon tired of the constant round of exercises; some were posted to commando units and other special services, where they were trained with a view to parachuting into occupied Norway and working with the Resistance. Not least after the Normandy invasion many were anxious to play an active role. Most of them, however, were told that they would comprise the reserve force for the actual liberation of Norway.

As time passed disappointment and despondency spread, as the men realised that they would not be actively deployed. There were continuous reports of the achievements of their fellow countrymen in the air force and navy, while they themselves remained idle in Scotland. Many felt they had been tricked. This was not what they had joined up for.

During the first few years of the war all military personnel were obligated to carry gasmasks, even on leave, but gradually these regulations were allowed to lapse.

A Brigade welfare officer was in charge of providing the various units and detachments with entertainment. There were visits and performances by Norwegian artists, films were shown, and lectures organised. The Brigade chaplain conducted services every Sunday in one of the local churches. He was an eloquent preacher. Our liaison officer, an elderly Scots colonel, often attended these services in order to hear our padre: he thought he spoke so beautifully. But our Scot didn't understand a single word.

His name was Sir John Aird. He had served as Crown Equerry under King Edward VIII, and had ridden beside the King down the Mall in the winter of 1936 when an attempt had been made on the life of the Monarch. Sir John had hurled himself between the King and his assailant, and probably saved his life.

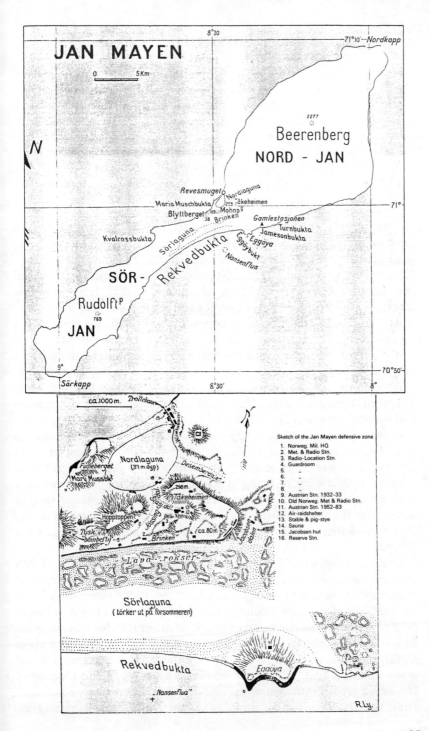

JAN MAYEN

0   5 Km

N

71°10'·· Nordkapp

2277

Beerenberg

NORD - JAN

71°

Revesmuget
Maria Muschbukta   Nordlaguna
   Blyttberget 169 Mohnp ⁹ Tåkeheimen
    38 Brinken
      Gamlestasjonen
Kvalrossbukta   Sörlaguna   Turnbukta
     Rekvedbukta   Jamesonbukta
      Eggöya
     Eggöbukt
    Nansenflua

SÖR -

Rudolft ᴾ
769

JAN

9°   70°50'

Sörkapp   8°30'   8°

ca. 1000 m.   Trollslia

Fugleberget
Mary Mussbkt

Nordlaguna
(31 m. dyp)

Desember-aja

298 m.

Tåkeheimen

Hopptoppen

Tysk.
bömbelly   Brinken   ca. 80 m.

Lava-rokser

Sörlaguna
(törker ut på forsommeren)

Rekvedbukta   Eggöya

„Nansenflua"

R.ly.

Sketch of the Jan Mayen defensive zone

1. Norweg. Mil. HQ.
2. Met. & Radio Stn.
3. Radio-Location Stn.
4. Guardroom
5.   „
6.   „
7.   „
8.   „
9. Austrian Stn. 1932–33
10. Old Norweg. Met & Radio Stn.
11. Austrian Stn. 1952–83
12. Air-raidshelter
13. Stable & pig-stye
14. Sauna
15. Jacobsen hut
16. Reserve Stn.

London

In the autumn of 1942 I was posted to the staff of the Norwegian Director of Medical Services in London. At the same time I was to serve as garrison M.O. for military personnel. Tavistock House, near King's Cross Station, housed a medical centre. The Norwegian government had taken over the large building, which contained several Norwegian offices, as well as a doctor's surgery for seamen and an x-ray institute.

At Holland Park there was a Norwegian hospital, which dealt with less serious cases. Patients could also be treated at British hospitals or at Craiglockhart Hospital in Edinburgh; and—if necessary—there was a hospital for venereal disease at Barnton, likewise situated in Edinburgh.

Norwegian armed forces and civilian authorities had their offices in Kingston House, two large office blocks that the Norwegian government had bought just south of Hyde Park.

Gunnar Johnson had been appointed Director of Medical Services in July 1941. Hearing that Professor Johan Holst had escaped from Norway and was in Stockholm, he managed to get Holst flown to London with a view to being appointed in his place. This was duly effected in November of that year. Holst had been professor of surgery at the Rikshospital in Oslo, and, together with Carl Semb, was the leading authority on the surgical treatment of pulmonary tuberculosis in Norway.

During the Spring of 1943 trouble was obviously brewing in the DMS staff, and soon came to a head. Leiv Kreyberg, who had been professor of pathology at the Rikshospital, had joined the staff. Those already on the staff included Kaare Poulsson and—as already mentioned—Gunnar Johnsson. These three presented a united front against Holst, insisting tht he was far too autocratic and failed to take the others into his confidence: furthermore that he had failed to devote sufficient time and energy to the question of developing the medical service with a view to the re-conquest of Norway, a problem with which they themselves were especially concerned. Holst was also criticised for devoting so much of his time to pulmonary tuberculosis operations at Newlands as well as at Craiglockhart, the two Norwegian hospitals, leaving him allegedly insufficient time to attend to his job as DMS. To this Holst replied that it was important to keep up his professional skills and knowledge. His critics submitted their complaints in a letter to the Supreme Command, concluding that a new DMS should be appointed, but nothing came of it.

It was not really surprising that Kreyberg's letter failed to achieve the desired result. He was a very enterprising and colourful individual, but was apt to express himself somewhat injudiciously. Once he had decided to champion a cause, he would brook no opposition, and he minced no words in his description of the top brass. When this came to their ears, the whole rumpus nearly ended in a court-martial. Fortunately Gunnar Johnsson came to the rescue. . . .

Holst was anxious that Norwegian surgeons should be sent to the various theatres of war to enable them to acquire some experience of wartime surgery.

In June 1944 Kreyberg, Johnsson and Poulsson were transferred, while Holst remained DMS until February 1945, when he handed over to Dr Carl Semb from Ullevaal Hospital, who had been flown over from Sweden.

Professor Kreyberg spent much of the first war years travelling round in the U.S.A., where, among other things, he worked on the development of concentrated rations for use in the field. This resulted in the mass production of the famous K ration, used by all Allied troops in various theatres of war (K for Kreyberg). He also collected funds for the equipping of medical and surgical units to be used in the liberation of Norway. These proved of inestimable value during the reconquest of Finnmark, Norway's northernmost county, in the autumn of 1944, when the retreating Germans carried out a scorched earth policy. They were driven back by Russian troops assisted by Norwegian units from Scotland and Norwegian contingents which had been training in Sweden thinly disguised as "police" units.

In May 1945 Kreyberg and Johnsson were sent by the Norwegian Supreme Command to North Norway, where they were to alleviate the plight of the many thousands of inmates of German prison camps living under appalling, sub-human conditions, as well as the Norwegian civilian population, most of whom were homeless as a result of the devastation inflicted by the retreating Germans. Already in the autumn of '44 Johnsson had been active in this part of Norway, assisting people who had suffered at the hands of the enemy. He had distinguished himself in particular during the evacuation of the inhabitants of Sørøya.

Kaare Poulsson had been one of my unit M.O.'s in Scotland. He was in fact the ardent motor-cyclist already mentioned, who was involved in an accident, and had to be rushed to hospital in Edinburgh with a collapsed lung. After leaving the staff of the DMS he was posted to STS*26, the Norwegian S.O.E. training establishment, underwent a parachute training course, and in the autumn of 1944 was dropped in the Aadalen area to work with the resistance, or Home Front, as they were known in Norway.

Conflicting views on work and planning were by no means confined to the office of the DMS. They were also in evidence in other departments of the armed forces, and were very much a result of the special conditions in which we lived.

In the end plans for the reconquest of Norway proved to be of minor significance: Norway was to be liberated on other fronts.

In the Royal Norwegian Navy the medical department had a doctor based in Liverpool. A few doctors and medical students also served on board Norwegian-manned destroyers which were heavily committed to the protection of trans-Atlantic convoys, as well as participating in the Normandy invasion, where one of the destroyers was lost.

The air force had a unit M.O. in each fighter squadron. These planes protected Allied bombers in their raids on the Continent. They also participated in the invasion of Normandy, playing their part in the Allied advance into the heart of Europe and had their own M.O. Knut Blaaflat. In all parts of the forces there was excellent co-operation between Norwegian and British medical services, and with the local hospitals, wherever we happened to be stationed.

---

*STS = Special Training School. Some of these were holding establishments for separate nationalities, e.g. French, Belgian, Polish, etc.; others were specialists training centres to which groups could be sent.

The war in Svalbard (Spitsbergen)

In May 1943 the DMS asked me if I was willing to join an expedition to Svalbard. I accepted straight away. As this was a hush-hush job I was given no details, but told to be prepared to set off at short notice. Johnsson advised me to take a shotgun, as there would be plenty of chances to get some good shooting. I got hold of a suitable weapon from a local gunsmith, and also bought a 16 mm camera and some colour film.

On the evening of May 29th I took the night train to Glasgow, and next morning drove to Greenock on the Clyde, where our expedition assembled. We were then split up into two parties, each one assigned to one of two cruisers lying in the Firth, the "Cumberland" and the "Bermuda". I was allotted to the former. We rode at anchor all day and had plenty of time to find our bearings. A number of other naval units were scattered around—aircraft carriers, battleships, destroyers and corvettes.

At 1300 hours on May the 31st we weighed anchor and headed down the Firth of Clyde, a veritable fleet in open formation, rounding the Mull of Kintyre and shaping a course for Iceland. All the way we had sunshine and a calm sea. Both cruisers were escorted by a destroyer or corvette on each side, two vigilant hounds on the lookout for U-boats. We made good speed, and far astern we caught a glimpse of the aircraft-carrier "Furious" with her escort. We were on a course that would take us along the west coast of Iceland to Akureyri in the north.

Our cruiser had a full complement. A number of the ratings had to sleep in hammocks slung in the corridors, as they had very hospitably given up their bunks to our party. We got on well with officers and men, and enjoyed very good fare in the mess. The chief surgeon on board, Ronald Kennedy, MRCS, showed me round his well-equipped sick bay, with its consulting room, operating theatre and hospital ward. The state of health on board was excellent, and there were no repercussions from shore leave.

Now at last we were told in detail what our task was: we were to take over from the "Fritheim" expedition, which had been sent to Svalbard a year previously, but had been attacked by German bombers which had killed and wounded many of its members. The wounded had been subsequently taken off by plane and brought back to the U.K. I had met them in the Edinburgh hospital, but never found out what had happened. They were bound to secrecy.

Our expedition consisted in the main of a platoon from the Brigade reconnaissance unit in Scotland under the command of Captain Trond Vigtel. It also included some navy personnel. The overall commander of the expedition was a naval captain, Peter Bredsdorff, who had been appointed governor of Svalbard. The code-name of our operation was "Gearbox IV".

Akureyri was reached in the afternoon of June 3rd. About a year after I had inspected the Norwegian military station there. Now it no longer existed.

For security reasons we were not allowed to land. We lay off Akureyri for several days, waiting for favourable ice conditions at Svalbard. Reports suggested that Grønnfjorden (Green Harbour), which we were to enter, was still ice-bound. In addition there was a great deal of drifting ice off the coast and inside Isfjorden (Ice Fjord). The "Cumberland" was under the command of Captain Maxwell-Hyslop, R.N. We had not seen him on the crossing from Scotland, as Action Stations was the rule at sea, which meant that everybody on watch had to be at his post. Enemy units might appear at any moment, and it was particularly important to be on the lookout for U-boats. Life on board was hemmed in by restrictions; there was, inter alia, a ban on the serving of alcohol.

Now that we were safe and sound in harbour, we could relax. The day after our arrival there was a formal dinner in the wardroom, with the captain presiding. As we enjoyed an excellent meal accompanied by assorted drinks we soon discovered that the captain was a genial and entertaining host. Among the parlour games played after dinner was an obstacle race won by the captain: this involved creeping through the service hatch into the galley, through corridors and back to the wardroom. Last man was promptly debagged to the accompaniment of loud cheers, not least from the loser himself.

We left Akureyri in the evening of June 7th, by which time Grønnfjorden was no longer ice-bound. We saw several naval units of varying size off the coast, and were later told that we were part of a plan to entice German warships from the fjords of North Norway, from which they launched constant attacks on the Murmansk convoys. We were the bait, while major naval forces lurked in the background, ready to go into action. In fact, there had been little effort made in investing our expedition with too much secrecy. Anyway, if that had really been the plan, it failed. The Germans stayed put.

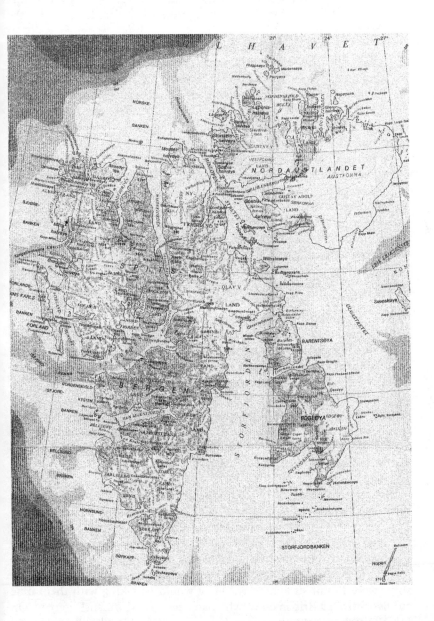

41

The voyage to Svalbard took about two and a half days. The weather remained reasonably good, with the wind only occasionally reaching strong breeze. The nights were now lighter, and before long we saw the midnight sun. Early on the morning of 10th June we caught sight of Svalbard with its jagged peaks and shimmering white glacier in between. Before noon we had reached the mouth of Isfjorden (Ice Fjord) where we were met by floes of drifting ice. To port lay Prince Carl's Foreland, and beyond Forlandsundet followed by Daumannsodden (Dead Man's Headland), a great flat expanse, only just visible above the surface of the sea and stretching away into the distance. It certainly deserves its name; many ships have gone aground here.

To starboard we have Cape Linné with Isfjord radio, now no longer in operation. Tall aerial masts rear up above a cluster of huts lying over a precipitous coast. A little further inland, towards the mountains, lies Lake Linné.

Further in we rounded the Festningsodden headland, and entered Grönnfjorden, which runs due south. Across the fjord, a little further south lies Barentsburg, the Russian coalmining settlement. On the opposite side, at the mouth of Grønnfjorden stands Cape Heer, commanding excellent views up Isfjorden to the east and westward to the entrance, in fact a strategically important point.

We reached Barentsburg at about 1300 hours GMT. The settlement is situated on a slope, which is steepest at its foot, flattening out on top to an inclined plane up to the entrance of the mine workings. The heaps of coal, lying down the slope near the shore, were still burning, almost two years after they had been set on fire when the settlement was evacuated. The installations and some of the buildings had been destroyed. Only a skeleton remained of the large office building. Patches of snow were still lying in between the houses. On the quay stood a large warehouse.

Owing to the ever-present danger of U-boats the cruiser with its escort lay off some distance from the land: it was vital to retain manoeuvrability.

Men and equipment were speedily landed, while personnel due for relief were embarked. The "Bermuda" was to continue up Isfjorden to Longyearbyen, where more personnel were to be relieved. I was met on the quay by the M.O. I had come to relieve, Per Hønningstad, who conducted me to the surgery and sick bay in the uppermost barrack. He was in a hurry to go on board, and I was only given a brief run-down; the ships were to sail straightaway. They would be taking with them nine survivors from a British crew, who had been in a Murmansk convoy. On 5th November, 1942, their ship "Chumleigh" had lost her bearings and grounded near South Cape, in the extreme south of Svalbard, where they were attacked by a flight of German bombers, setting their ship on fire. On the radio the captain was ordered to abandon ship and make his way to Isfjorden where there was said to be a Norwegian military outpost.

The shipwrecked crew set off in two lifeboats along the coast to the north. One boat disappeared with all hands. The other contained twenty-four all told. By the time they finally reached the entrance to Isfjorden four had frozen to death, and the remainder were so exhausted that they no longer had the strength to row, even though they could see the fire from the burning heaps of coal at Barentsburg. However, the current carried them to Cape Linné, where they just had enough strength to break their way into a hut which contained provisions. Several similar huts had been set up around Barentsburg, and were intended to provide a refuge in the event of attack. The next day some of them tried to go to Barentsburg, but were too weak for the deep snow. Death by freezing took a further toll; others died of gangrene, and finally their store of provisions ran out.

On New Year's Day of 1943 they were found by two men from Barentsburg who were out checking their fox traps. When they came near the hut they heard noises inside and thought it might be Germans. One man approached the door while the other sat down on a snow-covered heap to cover him. When he took a closer look he was surprised to find that he was sitting on the frozen body of a man. The floor of the hut presented a fearful sight: dead and dying were scattered around, and the stench of gangrenous wounds assailed the nostrils. The survivors, nine men, were brought to Barentsburg, where they were placed in the sick bay.

Now that they were leaving they were in good shape, even though some of them had had toes amputated. Their one overriding wish was to get home.

In 1946 the graves of those who had perished at Cape Linné were visited by the British Army Grave Service. They were all identified, and their remains transferred to Tromsø Cemetery. In 1946 a Norwegian whaler came across human remains on Dun Island on the west coast not far from South Cape, possibly the remains of the crew of the other lifeboat.

The "Cumberland" with her escort was soon on her way out of the fjord, accompanied after a while by the ships from Longyearbyen, and had soon disappeared behind Cape Linné.

We took stock of our surroundings. There was slush and mud all round. In the uppermost barrack furthest to the north, apart from a doctor's surgery and sick bay, there were offices and governor's quarters. A dentist, A. Syrrist by name, also lived here. In a building further down the slope there was a joint officers' and other ranks' mess. In the north-east corner of this cluster of buildings, beside a number of tall masts, stood a British research station, where ionospheric investigations were being carried out under the supervision of Lieutenant I. D. Watson, who also acted as liaison officer. The actual radio station comprised a rather insignificant-looking little hut with a relatively short aerial. It was situated close to a mine entrance at the top of the settlement, behind a large heap of coal. It was to play a major role in our defence of the place.

A few kilometres further south lay Finneset, the site of an important whaling station at the beginning of this century. It was here, too, that Svalbard's first radio station was set up in 1911. There was now a power station there.

Isfjord Radio at Kapp Linné started operating in 1934.

At Cape Heer some four kilometres north of Barentsburg, there was a garrison of ten. Their heaviest piece of ordnance was a four-inch gun plus a 20 mm Oerlikon anti-aircraft gun. It was reached along a length of rail previously used for the transport of coal from Grumant, a mining town further in Isfjorden.

The Barentsburg arsenal comprised a four-inch gun down on the northern slope, 2 Bofors 40 mm anti-aircraft guns, one of which was sited at the forward end of the heap of coal in front of the radio hut. In addition there was an Oerlikon, and machine guns.

In the warehouse on the quay we discovered a large number of Russian-type cigarettes with cardboard mouthpieces. There was also a considerable quantity of candy, which made our dentist wonder whether their personnel had also included a dentist. My medical corporal was a very able person by the name of Bjarne Kristiansen: he proved a great help in the surgery, supervising patients and assisting in checking on sanitary conditions. After a while I set about checking on the general state of health.

A few days later I visited Longyearbyen. Two motorboats had been made available, and half-way there we passed Grumantbyen, a minor Russian mining settlement on a steep slope, which also bore obvious signs of destruction. Operations here were discontinued in 1962.

Hotelneset at the mouth of the Advent Fjord was defended by 11 men, armed with a four-inch gun, as well as a number of small arms. Four kilometres further up we reached Longyearbyen. Beyond lies a valley containing Sverdrupbyen, two kilometres further in. There was a doctor's surgery here and a sickbay, run by a medical sergeant, T. Kaupang, an efficient deputy with a variety of skills. He could call me up from Barentsburg if there was anything out of the ordinary involved.

Longyearbyen too was the scene of burning heaps of coal and shattered installations. Officers and other ranks were quartered in the actual town, where there were living quarters, office buildings, canteens and a small chapel. Up on the slopes on either side of the valley the mine openings yawned. Local defence included a 40 mm Bofors anti-aircraft gun and machine-guns.

A whole string of sledge-dogs, for the most part Samoyeds and Greenland huskies, greeted our arrival. These splendid animals were used in winter to maintain communications between Barentsburg and Sveagruva, where there was a small manned outpost.

On the floor of the valley, behind Sverdrupbyen, was a steep rocky scree, which had to be negotiated on one's way up to the top. To the west this is followed by a gradual rise in the direction of Nordenskjöld fjell, from the top of which there were panoramic views of the whole of Svalbard and Nordaustlandet. That day the weather was on my side, and I enjoyed sweeping views of distant mountains and glaciers, and of the ocean far away to the west, taking it in on my camera. I was less fortunate on the way down, stumbling in the steep scree and breaking a couple of ribs, which continued to pester me for a couple of weeks.

Adventdalen is a broad, flat valley, running south-east to Sassendalen, the realm of the legendary Hilmar Nøis, a trapper who spent many a winter in Svalbard.

Captain Ernst Ullring of the Royal Norwegian Navy, who had been in Iceland in 1940–42, was being relieved of his post as Governor of Svalbard, after holding the appointment ever since his arrival with the relief expedition the previous summer. He was now putting his successor Bredsdorff in the picture.

A brief account of how Norway came to acquire these remote northern territories might be of use at this juncture.

In 1194 the Norwegian king Sverre Sigurdson despatched a small fleet of longboats on a voyage of discovery to the north from Iceland. They reached a country they called Svalbard, literally the land of the cold coasts. This event is well documented in old Icelandic writings, where the description and the position tally with the actual facts. King Sverre annexed this new country, but little more is heard of Svalbard before its discovery by the Dutch some 400 years later.

During the years 1594–1595 William Barentz set off, with the backing of Dutch merchants, to find a northern sea-route to China. The captain of his vessel was Jacob van Heemskerck, who later made several voyages to India. In 1607 he was appointed Admiral in Command of the Netherlands Navy, and won a great victory over the Spanish fleet at Gibraltar in 1607, though he lost his life in the battle.

Two years running Barentz encountered impenetrable ice, but in 1596 he set off with two ships, with J. C. Rijp in command of one. On board they carried a cargo of goods which they intended to exchange for spices, once they had reached their goal. First they reached Bear Island, so named because here they shot a huge polar bear. Sailing on they discovered a land of jagged peaks rising up between glaciers, and to this they gave the name Spitsbergen or Sharp Mountains. Returning to Bear Island the two ships parted company, Barentz with a crew of fifteen and Heemskerck as his skipper, steering a course to the east and arriving at Novaya Zemlja. Rounding its north point they reached the Kara Sea at the end of August and found it blocked with ice. Their ship was frozen fast in the ice off a bay on the east coast at about 76 degrees latitude N, which was given the name Ice Harbour. Having failed a few weeks later to break free from the ice, they were forced to spend the winter ashore. They brought with them the lifeboats and built a large hut of drift timber from Siberia.

A plentiful stock of polar bear kept them supplied with meat, as well as fat to produce oil for their lamps, while wood washed up on the beach gave them fuel for heating. In the middle of winter polar bears made themselves scarce, but were replaced by polar fox. With the coming of spring, however, the bear re-appeared. A high standard of hygiene was maintained, and a bathtub was made out of a wine barrel.

The months of total darkness, with temperatures of minus 50 degrees Centigrade, compelled them to remain indoors, which imposed a considerable strain, but when the light gradually returned at the end of January, and they could venture outside, their spirits rose. However, symptoms of scurvy gradually made themselves felt owing to the lack of vitamin C in their fare.

As late as June their ship was still stuck fast in the ice. As a last resort they raised the gunwhales on their lifeboats, and set off, alternately rowing and sailing, to cover the 1600 miles back to the Kola Peninsula. At times they had to drag their boats across the ice in order to make any progress. On the way Barentz and one of his men died of scurvy. In a state of extreme exhaustion they finally reached Kola, where they met Rijp, who had brought his ship all the way back from Holland in order to find them.

Gerrit de Veer, who had joined the expedition as its chronicler, compiled a detailed log of the voyage. Nearly 300 years later, in 1871, the Dutchmen's hut was found, completely covered with ice, by a Norwegian, Elling Carlsen, and in 1875 Gardener found Barentz's own diary.

The Dutch came across abundant stocks of whale in these northern waters, and large-scale whaling operations were started around Svalbard. They set up a land-based station on Amsterdam Island in the north-west corner of the archipelago, where they produced whale oil.

The English, loth to be outsmarted by their arch rivals at sea, were soon to make their presence felt.

The English polar explorer Henry Hudson had also discovered Svalbard in 1607 when he was sent out to find the North-West Passage. He reached the west coast of Svalbard and Whale Bay, and found plentiful stocks of whale in all these waters. It gave an extra stimulus to English whaling. The next year he was sent on another expedition to find the North-East Passage, but came only as far as to Novaya Zemlja as ice in the Kara Sea stopped further progress. In 1610 he went on an expedition to the west and discovered Hudson Bay where he spent the winter. Badly prepared for this and with difficult ice conditions in the summer there was a mutiny on board; he and his son with several of the crew were left in an open boat to a certain death.

*In 1611 the English Moscovy Company started whaling up there, having previously hunted walrus around Bear Island. At first the company appears to have paid tribute to the Dano-Norwegian king. In 1613 when clashes occurred between the English and Dutch whalers, the company urged the English king, James I, to grant them a monopoly. An offer by the king to buy the islands failed to elicit any response from Copenhagen, whereupon the king occupied Svalbard by royal declaration of British supremacy over the islands, giving the company the sole right to whaling in the area. The occupation was marked by a small ceremony in Magdalena Bay in 1614, attended by the company's whaling skippers, headed by Robert Fotherby. A cross was erected with the royal Coat-of-Arms.

Holland protested, and the occupation was not accepted by any other nation except France. Eventually the English and Dutch whalers agreed to divide the area between them.

As stocks of whale were gradually depleted, the English withdrew more than fifty years later, leaving the Dutch to continue for many a long year. Later they were joined by the Norwegians. These started, together with the Russians, hunting and trapping some two hundred years ago. Towards the end of last century the Norwegians started coalmining in Svalbard. Søren Zachariassen brought the first shipment to Tromsø in 1899. Mining companies were organised and other nations came on the scene: British, Americans, Swedish and Russian mines were opened, but of these only the Russian and Norwegian companies persisted, as the others found the undertaking rather unremunerative. The American John Longyear had started the Arctic Coal Company in Longyearbyen in 1906, but sold it in 1916 to the Norwegians giving his name to the place.

---

*Martin Conway: No Man's Land.

In 1920 Norway was granted sovereign rights over Svalbard in accordance with the treaty of that year, and entered officially into possession of the archipelago on 1st August, 1925. The signatory powers were to enjoy the right to exploit its natural resources, but all military activity was banned.

The first person to negotiate the North-East Passage was the well-known Swedish polar explorer Adolf Erik Nordenskjöld who sailed through to the Bering Straits in 1878–79 on the steamer "Vega," captained by naval Ltn. Palander. He was accompanied by three other ships and a scientific team from several nations. He had earlier led expeditions to Svalbard. After the occupation of Norway it seemed as if the Germans had no intention of intervening in Svalbard, although they may have had plans to extend the mining of coal for the extraction of petrol, and also of establishing a garrison. But this would have meant earmarking troops for the defence of the islands, and this hardly seemed worth while. Besides, as well as getting coal, they were also getting weather reports, and these were to prove every bit as important as coal.

To start with the people living in Svalbard were very uneasy, not knowing what would happen. Many of them were anxious to return to Norway, but after a while their anxiety subsided, and people settled down.

Their first contact with the Germans was in April 1941, a year after the invasion on the mainland. During a serious fire in a mine in Longyearbyen several workers were killed. The mine manager Finn Boger appealed for help to Einar Sverdrup, Managing Director of the Norwegian Spitsbergen Coal-Mining Company in Oslo, with a request for much needed fire-fighting equipment, masks and oxygen. Sverdrup thereupon approached the German authorities, who dispatched planes with rescue equipment to Svalbard, which was still ice-bound.

With the help of the equipment that was sent up, the fires were put out and mining operations re-started. At the end of July the first collier was able to leave for Norway.

Later on voices were raised in protest at these Norwegian efforts to procure coal for occupied Norway.

In his diary the most experienced of the German arctic pilots Schütze describes his first visit to the islands and the flying conditions he encountered. The day before another pilot had flown up in bright sunshine, and dropped supplies without any problem. The very next day Schütze found Svalbard covered in clouds with a ceiling of 1000 metres, which meant that his charts were of little use. However, here and there mountain tops poked through the clouds, and with the aid of a Baedeker map he was able to recognise the peaks he saw, and to some extent find his bearings, while at the same time comparing his altimeter readings with the spot-heights shown on the map. Spiralling down through a hole in the clouds, he discovered by referring to the map, that he was over Bell Sound, some 50 km south of Longyearbyen. He spiralled back up and continued north. A fresh gap showed him that he was over Isfjorden. When he suddenly cut through cloud base he caused such panic among the seals on the ice that they scuttled for the shelter of their blow-holes. But unfortunately there were not enough holes to go round, and when several at a time tried the same hole they were clustered together with heads down and tails up.

Schütze had orders to drop the equipment by parachute, but when one of the 'chutes failed to open he decided to land, as he still had the oxygen cylinders on board. He glided down to a runway that had been prepared on the ice, even though it was rather short. On touching down he discovered that the wall of snow on either side was higher than anticipated. As a result one of his wings dug in, his plane slewed round and he landed far out in loose snow. People came running up from every quarter and dug him out while the governor prepared to welcome him, and to thank him for landing. The day before oxygen cylinders had been smashed when a 'chute failed to open. Willing hands helped to dig out the plane and extend the runway, so that he could take off. His plane, a Heinkel 111, with a crew of four, was the first German aircraft to land in Svalbard. On their return flight they carried over a hundred scraps of paper, inscribed with messages, from the many witnesses to this landing and intended for friends and relatives in Norway. When they landed at Værnes outside Trondheim, they had a busy time addressing and mailing these letters.

As pilot of a "met. plane" Schütze had already flown westwards from Værnes in the direction of the Faroes, Iceland, Jan Mayen and Greenland. In November 1940 he had suddenly emerged from cloud cover at a low height above Reykjavik to be met with intense anti-aircraft flak from land and naval vessels in the harbour, and was forced to take refuge in a cloud.

On 24th March, 1941, he was ordered to fly to East Greenland and back, a distance of 1700 km. He set off in a Heinkel 111 fitted with reserve fuel tanks and a crew of four. After flying for 600 km he flew into a great dark cloud from which there appeared to be no escape. His plane started to ice up, and suddenly it was struck by lightning. His windscreen was shattered, and he was knocked half unconscious, and at the same time feels the full force of a hailstorm striking his face at a speed of 300 km an hour, blinding him completely. His goggles are iced up and are of no use. His navigator holds up a mapcase to shield his face, and he tries to peer out between his fingers. The temperature in the cockpit drops suddenly to minus 25, and with a great effort Schütze manages to dive down to warmer air, and to turn back. But the altimeter has packed up, and the two compasses give different readings. Fortunately he manages to get a bearing from Trondheim radio beacon, and made it to Værnes, somewhat the worse for wear and with a minor eye injury.

A week later, fully restored, he took off once more. The weather was now good, and after flying for $4\frac{1}{2}$ hours he was over Scoresby Sound in brilliant sunshine. He flew low over the settlement, which consisted of 20 houses. The inmates hoisted the Danish flag, and waved. Off the coast huge icebergs glinted in the sun. After circling round for half an hour he turned and flew back.

Shortly afterwards, in May 1941, a dramatic event took place, when eight men seized the icebreaker "Isbjørn", which was employed in keeping the channel open in Isfjorden in the spring and autumn. The captain and the chief engineer, both suspected of Nazi sympathies, were locked in their cabins.

The captors shaped a course for Iceland, but halfway there the engine broke down, probably owing to sabotage on the part of the engineer, and they were forced to hand over control—as well as their arms—and suffer the indignity of being, in their turn, locked up. The boat was now set on a course for Svalbard. Shortly afterwards they met a Russian boat on its way to England. The prisoners asked to be taken on board, but the captain refused, insisting that they must return and atone for their crime. He informed Svalbard of what had happened.

The governor Marlow and the mine manager Einar Sverdrup were faced with a dilemma: what should they do? If the authorities in Norway were informed, this might prove fatal to the eight captors. On the other hand it was feared that the Germans might get to know of the incident and carry out reprisals. In the end a report was sent to Tromsø, and a patrol boat was despatched to fetch the prisoners. Back in Tromsø the Gestapo were waiting, and after the usual round of torture six of them were condemned to death and executed. After the people living in Svalbard had been evacuated to Britain a charge was brought against the administration, but the matter was dropped. The captain, however, was sentenced to a term of imprisonment. In the opinion of some of the members of the Norwegian government in exile in London, he should have been sentenced to death.

In the summer of 1941 several conferences were held in London, attended by Norwegian, British and Russian representatives, to decide what to do with Svalbard. There were three Norwegian mining settlements in the archipelago, Longyearbyen, Sveagruva and Ny-Aalesund (Kings Bay), and three Russian, Barentsburg, Grumant and Pyramiden tucked away at the head of the Billefjorden. The aim was to deny the Germans access to stocks of coal, from which they could produce petrol.

Bringing the coal to Britain would require setting up a convoy service, and this would not be worth the trouble; besides every ship available was employed in protecting the convoys. Russia having been drawn into the war against Germany in June 1941.

A month later, on 22nd July, the British cruiser "Nigeria," accompanied by the destroyer "Punjab," arrived off Svalbard under the command of Admiral Sir Philip Vian, hero of the so-called "Altmark" affair, when the German boat of that name was intercepted in Norwegian coastal waters, and her human cargo of British merchant sailors liberated. Apart from discovering if there were any Germans in Svalbard, Sir Philip's task was to investigate the possibility of establishing a base. For security reasons the Norwegian authorities were not informed. The task force, however, included a Norwegian naval officer, Lieut. Ragnvald Tamber, who had formerly served in these parts.

A landing was made at Cape Linné, at the mouth of Isfjorden where Isfjord Radio station was situated, but there was no trace of any Germans. At Longyearbyen a commando force under Lieutenant-Colonel Godfrey went ashore. Governor Marlov protested, but he and the manager of the mining company, Einar Sverdrup, had to resign themselves to the fact that Ragnvald Tamber would take over as Governor. He would ensure that no messages were transmitted to Norway, and a similar order was also issued to the Russians of no transmission in their three mining settlements at Barentsburg, Grumantbyen and Pyramiden. On the return voyage to Britain Sir Philip's task force, in accordance with orders, destroyed the German meteoro- logical station on Bear Island.

The conclusion reached by this expedition was that establishing a base for the defence of Svalbard would involve too many problems. Instead it was decided to evacuate the inhabitants.

Accordingly on 24th August a force arrived outside Isfjorden consisting of the cruisers "Nigeria" and "Aurora," together with the troop transport "Empress of Canada," under the command of Rear-Admiral L. Vian, carrying a mixed detachment of troops comprising 25 Norwegians, a number of Russians, and 650 Canadians commanded by the Canadian Brigadier A. E. Potts. The Norwegian contingent was under the command of Major Aage Pran, who had been temporarily appointed O.C. troops, Svalbard. A little later a tanker escorted by 4 armed trawlers arrived.

The next morning after aerial reconnaissance had been carried out over Isfjorden in order to establish the presence or otherwise of German troops, the "Empress of Canada" entered Grønnfjorden with a view to embarking the Russians in Barentsburg. Together with the inhabitants of the other two Russian settlements at Grumant and Pyramiden, who had already been fetched, the number of people to be embarked amounted to as many as 2175.

Brigadier Potts went ashore with a detachment of troops and a representative from the Russian embassy in London and met with the Russian Consul who seemed to be co-operative. A Russian-speaking British officer was put in charge of bringing the people on board. Everything seemed to go smoothly. But when all but a couple of hundred had been safely brought on board, the Russian Consul refused to go. The British officer paid repeated visits to the consul's office in an attempt to make him change his mind, but to no avail. At every visit the officer was offered an assortment of choice Russian drinks of which the consul took copious draughts. As the time for departure approached both Brigadier Potts and Admiral Vian had a try, but in vain. The message from the Russian ambassador Maisky in London was not sufficient, and he put out a guard to stop more people going on board. As the officer saw the consul getting drunk he got the idea to urging him to take even more drinks. He finally passed out and disappeared under the table. Immediately two sailors appeared with a stretcher and carried him aboard followed by a furiously protesting vice consul.

The officer was shrewd enough to have the event photographed. When the Russians as expected subsequently lodged a complaint it was withdrawn when the photographic evidence was produced.

When the guard and the rest of the people saw the consul being carried on board they all followed without further trouble.

On board there weren't enough cabins and berths for everybody, which resulted in a good deal of disruption and squabbling about sleeping accommodation, so in the end the crew left them to find their own places. During the stormy journey to Arkangelsk women and men lay huddled in heaps in corridors and staterooms, and quite openly many took advantage of this proximity. The trip took four days with the ship pitching and tossing. General seasickness and blocked toilets soon turned the ship into a veritable pigsty. However, thanks to the stormy weather the U-boats kept away.

On the arrival at Arkangelsk the consul played the role of the contrite sinner, although this did not deter him from lodging a complaint.

The transports had cast anchor off the River Dvina, where 186 French and Belgian prisoners of war were embarked. These were men who had managed to escape from German prison camps and made their way into Poland, where they had been moved from one Russian prison to another, starved and neglected, and in rags by the time they came on board. While the British prisoners had been flown to England the remainder were now able to enjoy to the full the hospitality of their Canadian hosts.

On 1st September the ship returned to Grønnfjorden, and the

evacuation of the Norwegian settlers now began. The inhabitants of the other two mining communities at Ny Aalesund and Sveagruva at the head of the Van Mijenfjorden had been brought to Longyearbyen together with trappers from the various huts scattered about Svalbard. These, numbering some 800 were now sent to Grønnfjorden and taken on board the "Empress of Canada". About a hundred had preceded them. Three fully-laden colliers had been despatched to Iceland, with an escort, under the command of Lieutenant Tamber. On orders from London all plant and machinery were destroyed, and all stocks of coal set on fire, despite the vigorous protests of the governor and the manager of the Longyearbyen mining company, Mr Sverdrup. Over 200,000 tons of human toil literally went up in smoke, one more example of the senseless destruction of war.

The radio stations in Longyearbyen and at Cape Linné were dismantled just before departure, after operating up to the very last moment in order not to arouse the suspicions of the Germans. The weather reports broadcast made meteorological conditions sound a great deal worse than they really were, to ensure that no more ships were sent up.

Only one man stayed behind, a mine worker by the name of Halvorsen, who insisted that he was a pacifist, and refused to be sent to Scotland to carry out any form of military training. He managed to remain in hiding until everyone else had left, and when the Germans arrived later that autumn they took him back to Norway.

Operation "Gauntlet", as it was called, left Svalbard on 3rd September, and arrived in Greenock five days later. On their return voyage Rear-Admiral Vian with his cruisers had made a detour to the coast of Finnmark, launching an attack near North Cape on a German convoy consisting of two troop transports escorted by a destroyer and a number of smaller vessels. The destroyer was sunk, but owing to heavy seas and poor visibility the other ships escaped.

When the broadcasting of weather reports came to an end a German plane flew up on 5th September to investigate, only to discover burning stocks of coal and no sign of human life, apart from the lone pacifist, who waved in welcome. A few days later Canadian radio announced that the evacuation had been completed. The Germans immediately decided to establish a met. station "up there", and on 25th September a Junker 52 arrived carrying a detachment led by Dr Etienne, which proceeded to set up a provisional transmitter. This was followed by several plane-loads of material, and by early October the "Bansø" radio station was fully operative in Adventdalen. Dr. E. W. Etienne had been a member of the Oxford University East Greenland expedition in 1938, in the role of meteorologist. He was now the head of the German Air Force met. service in the north.

Co-operation between the German navy and the Luftwaffe was not always harmonious, and the former set up its own "Knospe" met. station at Krossfjorden that autumn.

The Germans realised that as soon as they started transmitting they might be located and attacked by the Allies. For this reason they immediately set to work to prepare a refuge to which they could retreat should need arise. Their fears were soon realised: only a few days later four RN minesweepers on their way back from Murmansk were ordered to proceed to Svalbard and deal with the situation. On 18th October two Luftwaffe transport planes Ju 52's were on their way from Banak in North Norway to Svalbard with extra equipment. Off Bear Island they spotted two ships, which they took to be destroyers, sailing north. Taking cover in a cloud they radioed news of this back, and then continued as planned. Next morning a Heinkel 111 flew over Isfjorden and spotted the two ships, which fired at the plane. Evacuation of the station was immediately started; a Ju 52 took off shortly after with 16 men from the station in Adventdalen.

The next one to take off was the Heinkel 111. By the time it was airborne the ships were already inside Adventfjorden. They opened fire, but without success. Now only one Ju 52 remained. It was compelled to await the arrival of the men from Longyearbyen, and when it finally tried to take off, one engine failed to start owing to the cold, and then caught fire. By the time the fire was put out the engine had been warmed up, and sprang into life. As luck would have it, too, the ships—now lying off Longyearbyen had failed to discover that there was still one more aircraft left. Visibility was poor, and the wind had created a dust cloud. Not till it was in the air was the plane spotted. The minesweepers opened up with their anti-aircraft guns, but missed.

On its way out the Heinkel 111 had spotted the other two minesweepers at the mouth of Isfjorden. It immediately flew back, and circled the runway until the last plane had taken off. All three aircrafts and their crews returned to Banak safe and sound. However, in the scramble to get away the last plane had left behind some luggage and a sheaf of secret documents. These were discovered by a patrol from the minesweepers which had been landed and ordered to submit "Bansö" radio station to a thorough search. The broadcasting equipment and all installations were destroyed, but the actual station building was allowed to stand.

Next day the Germans returned, rather hoping they could recover the documents they had left behind, only to be disappointed. However, they were delighted to find the building intact. New apparatus and equipment was flown up, and fourteen days later the station was fully operative, and continued sending throughout the winter with a team of four.

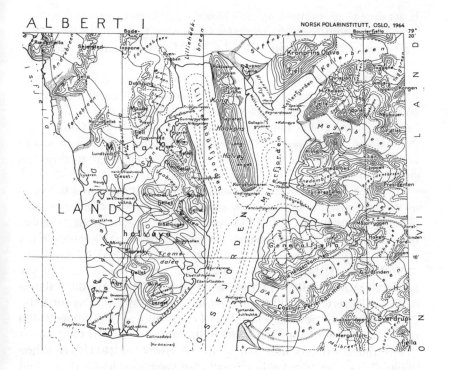

During the winter of 1941/1942 Hilmar Reksten, chairman of the board of directors of the Norwegian Spitsbergen Mining Company, lobbied Norwegian politicians in London in order to persuade the authorities to re-start mining in Svalbard. At the very least, he insisted, the mines should be overseen and maintained. This, however, was a matter of minor importance to the Allies: the decisive factor was to resume the weather-reporting service. For the Murmansk convoys this was vital. At the same time the German meteorological service should be stopped. It was then not known that the German navy had set up a station in Krossfjorden. This was identified in the spring of 1942.

In April 1942 it was decided to dispatch a Norwegian expedition. This was to be the prelude to what might be called the Svalbard Met. War. The operation was code-named "Fritham", and included two ships: the ice-breaker "Isbjørn" and the sealing vessel "Selis", manned by a total of about 60 men, all old Svalbard hands. The leader of the expedition was Einar Sverdrup, manager of the mining company in Longyearbyen, who for the occasion had been granted the rank of Lieutenant-Colonel, while a naval lieutenant, Øi, was in charge of military operations. The boats were to try to sneak up to Svalbard without an escort, as this might attract the attention of the powerful sea and air forces at the disposal of the enemy in North Norway. Besides, the Murmansk convoys needed all the escort vessels they could muster.

On 30th April the boats left Greenock for Akureyri in Iceland. Apart from small arms, their only means of defence consisted of anti-aircraft guns. On arrival Einar Sverdrup came on board together with the two liaison officers, Lieutenant-Colonel A. S. T. Godfrey and Commander A. R. Glen. Also Major A. S. Whatman, a radio specialist, who was to establish a station for ionospheric research, apart from the wireless station.

On 2nd April a Catalina had flown up to Svalbard and found Isfjorden in bright sunshine and seen no sign of any Germans there. A new reconnaissance flight on 2nd May had been prevented by bad weather from reaching its goal to give new information before the expedition left Iceland on the 5th May.

Not till later did the plane reach Svalbard, to discover that the Germans were installed. This occurred on 12th May, and the Catalina had been observed by the expedition as it sailed north. The pilot, Fl. Ltn. Healy, had spotted a Heinkel 111 parked on the snowcovered runway in Advent Valley and attacked it.

The four Germans who had spent the winter of 1941/1942 at the "Bansö" weather station in Adventdalen were due to be relieved in spring. When this could take place, however, was a problem: they would have to wait until the depth of snow had decreased sufficiently to permit landing and taking off on the ice. On the other hand it would never do to wait so long that the ice had started to break up, when a plane would face the risk of sinking through. Besides, at that stage Allied ships would be able to approach the station. When a report was received that one of the men was ill, it was immediately decided to take off, even though the snow was still rather deep on the runway where they now had to land. On 12th May Schütze set off from his base in North Norway in a Heinkel 111, with a full crew and a relief party of 6, with Dr. Etienne carrying a few boulders which would be dropped on the snow to test its consistency. They were accompanied by a Junker 88 whose role was to monitor the attempt. They arrived in a blaze of sunshine. The boulders dropped from the plane bounced and slithered along the snow. Would it be safe to land? He made a cautious attempt, his undercarriage streaking across the snow, which appeared to be firm. Taking off and circling he put the aircraft down carefully. All went well to start with, but all of a sudden his wheels sank through, and although he gave full throttle, the plane failed to rise. As a last resort he tried to make a runway by taxi-ing the plane up and down.

While this is going on they see a Catalina flying straight at them. They try to bring their machine-guns into action, but these are clogged with snow and refuse to fire. The plane makes a low-level approach, and the Germans scatter and go to ground in the snow. The Catalina completes a circuit, and makes a fresh approach, its machine-guns blazing. This is repeated ten times, and after every attack the Germans scatter further afield. Finally the Catalina flies off. The escorting Ju 88 had turned for home once Schütze had landed, and could not be contacted by radio. None of the crew had been hit, but the plane had been riddled with machine-gun fire: there were 30 bullet holes in the fuselage, and one engine and a fuel tank had been hit, but there appeared to be no leak. Anticipating the worst, Schütze enters the cockpit, and starts the engines, which respond perfectly. He taxis up and down, to extend the runway, and finally just manages to take off with the relieved party. Ice-cold draughts from all the holes in the fuselage stream into the cockpit, but these are soon plugged, and although there is an oil leak from one of the engines, he returns to base at Banak safe and sound. After repairs had been carried out, the plane was once again on its way to Svalbard six days later, landing on the ice. This time one wheel sinks through, and they are stuck fast, with their propeller damaged, and their plane has to be abandoned. A week later, when the Catalina pilot spots the plane still standing there; he assumes it's finished and refrains from attacking; but he has no idea that in the meantime it has flown to Norway and back. Not long after, the German plane goes to the bottom.

The German who had been reported sick turned out to be suffering from "polar sickness", a complaint brought on by the long dark winter months spent in confined quarters with the same companions, day after day. The patient becomes depressed and morose, and falls out with his fellows, creating problems. Personnel selected for service in these regions must be carefully vetted. The man in question had in fact taken another's place just before they started the previous autumn. Meeting new faces invariably cures the condition, and he had been the first to welcome Schütze, when the latter landed. Later on we were to come across a similar case, another German who was less fortunate, and there were a few cases in the Norwegian garrison that spent the 1942/43 winter in Svalbard.

The "Fritheim" expedition was not informed that there were Germans in Svalbard. Their wireless receiver was not powerful enough to pick up messages once the ships had left Iceland.

On the morning of 14th May the "Isbjørn" and "Selis" reached the entrance to Isfjorden to find it icebound. In clearing a channel they are forced to use dynamite, and progress is slow and time-consuming. Extra time is spent investigating Cape Linné to see if there are any Germans stationed there. They are spotted by a German reconnaissance plane on its way in, which immediately reports back to Norway. The Germans were under the impression that the boats were Russian, and that the Russians intended to establish themselves again in Barentsburg, thus posing a threat to the German station in Adventdalen. The same afternoon four German planes are ready to take off from Værnes air base.

Breaking the ice, which is particularly thick inside Grønnfjorden round Barentsburg, is a slow business. After about a day, with 1500 metres of channel still left to clear, four Fokke-Wulf Condors, flying low, approached from the south, and proceed to pepper the boats with their machineguns and are answered by anti-aircraft fire from the ships. The crews scatter across the ice, and seek cover behind hummocks of ice. The planes close in for a fresh attack, dropping bombs, some of which rebound from the ice and explode in the air. "Isbjørn" receives a direct hit and sinks in a matter of seconds together with all eleven on board, including Sverdrup and Godfrey. Onboard "Selis" gunner Nils Langbakk blazes away for dear life with his Oerlikon. A bull's eye! A Kondor disappears in flames, and another is winged. The German planes sheer off.

The "Selis" was on fire, burning for a whole day and night before she went down. Most of those on board had scattered across the ice, where they were machine-gunned. Two were killed outright, and ten badly wounded, one of whom died.

Sverdrup had suspended ice-breaking operations for five hours, as he was anxious to carry out a reconnaissance ashore. Lieutenant Øi protested at this decision: it was vital to get ashore as quickly as possible, as they had been spotted by a German plane. The upshot of it was that they failed to get ashore in time.

After Sverdrup had gone down with "Isbjørn" his second-in-command Lieutenant Roll-Lund was left in charge. The wounded were brought ashore and placed in a well-equipped sickbay that the Russians had left behind. Here Dr. Hönningstad set to work at once to attend to their needs, but he was very short of medicaments and other equipment that had gone down with the ships. Fortunately there were plenty of well-furnished beds, on which the exhausted men could relax after all the tension and exertion. As for food, they found an excellent supply of frozen pork in a snowdrift from pigs killed 9 months before when the place was evacuated.

As all the radio equipment had been lost when the ships went down, they had no contact with the outside world, and were unable to inform the U.K. of the course of events. They would have to wait eleven days as arranged, when a plane would arrive, if no word had been heard from them.

Two days after the above action Schütze flew over Barentsburg, and observed a number of ski tracks in the area, but none leading away from it, which led him to conclude that the station in Adventdalen was in no imminent danger. The Germans still believed that the new arrivals in Barentsburg were Russians.

During the next few days the Barentsburg settlement was bombed and machine-gunned by German planes, with no means of retaliation, as the anti-aircraft guns had gone down with the boats. Roll-Lund, fearing an attack by land-based forces, despatched some of his men to Svea and the surrounding huts and a detachment to defend Cape Heer, where Major Whatman and a wireless operator, Skribeland, were stationed.

The Allied Command in Britain knew what had happened in Svalbard. The German code had been broken by Enigma and reports from the Germans planes intercepted. They knew that the two ships had been sunk but nothing more of what had happened. They did not publish it so as not to let the Germans know that the code was broken.

The detachment sent to Sveagruva is under the command of Lieutenant Øi. On their way one of them, Odd Syvertsen, falls down a crevasse, landing on a ledge about 30 feet down. As they have no rope they improvise one by linking ski sticks together, fastening the hand straps to the baskets. Syvertsen clings to it, and the men haul him up carefully. Just before he reaches the top, sheer exhaustion forces him to relinquish his handhold, and he plunges down and lands on the same ledge, bruised and bloody and badly shaken. A fresh attempt is made, this time using belts in addition, which he can strap round his waist. Once again, just before reaching the top, a strap breaks, and once again he disappears into the depths, this time landing further down, battered and bruised. He calls out that they are to continue on their way, and in the face of this desperate situation, despite some misgivings, they do so. At Sveagruva they find rope, but when they make their way back they find that Syvertsen has disappeared in the depths below.

Roll-Lund's first concern was to establish if there were any Germans in Longyearbyen.

The first patrol was sent off already on the 16th May headed by Sergeant Rikard Knutsen on the 50 km long trip to Longyearbyen. The next day another patrol left led by Sergeant Østbye. They made only one ski track, keeping far apart in order to be less noticed from the air. But in spite of this the track was seen by a German airplane coming over. They threw themselves into the snow as the plane came nearer to investigate. It flew several times over without seeing them, thanks to their white camouflages and the shimmer in the snow from the sun. Arriving on the mountains above Longyearbyen, joining up with the other patrol they started watching the Germans down in the village and in Adventdalen where they had installed themselves. They discovered the radiostation "Bansø" in Adventdalen with its runway, and heard the sound of the generator down there which had puzzled them in the beginning. They reported back estimating the number of Germans higher than the actual number.

Their ski tracks were soon discovered and airplanes started criss-crossing the sky over them. But they were not detected as they were able to hide in the horizontal mines which they had known from childhood. Then they started making many more tracks to make the Germans believe there were many more of them. The Germans responded with renewed attacks on Barentsburg with machine guns and bombs. One of these fell unexploded close to the wall of the sickbay scaring the hell out of the patients. But two courageous men managed to remove it.

The trap seemed to have worked as the Germans left earlier than expected.

On 25th May Flight-Lieut. Dennis Healy in his Catalina arrives to look for them. He spots the bogged-down Heinkel 111 in Adventfjorden, and on his way back chances to see light signals coming from Cape Heer.

Wireless-Operator Skribeland had seized his Aldis lamp as soon as he spotted the plane, ready to make a signal. Major Whatman knocked it out of his hand. "It's a German plane", he yelled. "No, it's a Catalina", Skribeland assured him, retrieving his lamp and continuing to tap out his message. Healy signalled back, and put them at their ease with the information that there were far fewer Germans in Longyearbyen than anticipated; and in the meantime dropping some supplies. Lieut. Roll-Lund now started preparations for an attack on the enemy.

Healy subsequently made several trips, involving each time a flight of 24 hours or more from Sullum Voe in the Shetlands to bring much-needed weapons, ammunition and provisions. On 6th June he was barely able to bring his flying boat down among all the ice floes in Grønnfjorden and take off with the wounded.

German radio had announced the attack on the two ships the day after it had taken place, and had also claimed that naval vessels had been sunk, and for this reason the Admiralty in London were inclined to doubt the full truth of the report even if they knew about it. The facts were not known until Healy flew up after the agreed eleven days had elapsed on 25th May.

News of what had taken place in Svalbard provoked sharp reactions in London, and the idea of despatching a naval task force to drive out the Germans was mooted. In the end it was decided to despatch a relief expedition.

Operation "Gearbox 1" was led by Captain Ernst Ullring, and transported on board the cruiser "Manchester" and the destroyer

"Eclipse" under the command of Vice-Admiral Sir Cecil Bonham-Carter. Leaving Scapa Flow on 25th June, the force proceeds to Seydisfjord in Iceland, and after aerial reconnaissance to the north steams at full speed northward via Jan Mayen to Svalbard, alert to the threat of German naval units in North Norway and on their guard against U-boats. The relief of the Barentsburg garrison is rapidly completed. There is no time to attack the Germans in Longyearbyen. These had actually begun to withdraw. For the same reason a platoon of Norwegian paratroopers who had formed part of the task force are also brought back to the U.K.

The Germans carry out daily flights to Longyarbyen landing on the ice. But as the ice is breaking up a Heinkel gets stuck and finally sinks. As it is no longer possible to land on the ice a Junker tries to put down on the improvised runway near the station in Adventdalen, but the spring thaw makes it impossible to take off again, and Healy in his Catalina destroys it on the ground. Two aircrews marooned in Longyearbyen are fetched on 30th June, and on 9th July the last remaining Germans are evacuated. Before leaving they install the automatic meteorological transmitter Kröte (Toad), similar to several others set up in Svalbard.

Ullring establishes a garrison in both Barentsburg and Longyearbyen, leaving Roll-Lund in charge of the latter. Both detachments are now armed with anti-aircraft guns capable of keeping enemy planes at a respectful distance. On 21st July a Ju 88 had one engine put out of action over Barentsburg, but managed to limp back to Banak. Two days later another Junker takes off with the arctic explorer Dr. Etienne on board. Contact with the plane is lost, and it is assumed to have been shot down.

By air reconnaisance over the huts along Isfjorden the wreckage of the plane is found on the other side of Adventfjorden at Hjorthamn. It had been hit above Longyearbyen, and in attempting a forced landing had struck an overhead cable, killing all four onboard. The dead were buried here. Once again Nils Langbak was at the gun now taking revenge for his ship that was sunk.

German planes keep their distance, but U-boats are still a nuisance, setting houses in Barentsburg on fire with their guns. Ullring asks London to let them have bigger guns, and flies down in person to fetch three four-inch guns from the Norwegian destroyer Sleipner, which had been laid up. These arrive on 17th September with the expedition "Gearbox 2", which also brings reinforcements, motorboats and sledge-dogs on the cruisers "Cumberland" and "Sheffield". Once the guns have been installed at Barentsburg, Cape Heer and Hotelneset, and have fired a number of well-aimed shots, the U-boats keep well away.

On 16th October another taskforce, "Gearbox 3", arrives with reinforcements and provisions for the winter.

The primary task entrusted to our particular operation, "Gearbox 4", was to keep the UK supplied with weather reports. Vital munitions on their way to Murmansk had to be protected at all costs. If visibility was good, German reconnaissance planes could keep their U-boats informed; and it was just as vital for the Germans to prevent the convoys getting through, for which reason weather reports were of supreme importance for them too.

Our second task was consequently to prevent the Germans setting up meteorological stations. If they succeeded in doing so, it was our duty to destroy them, and for this reason we were a military unit, equipped for defence and attack.

In September 1942 Dennis Healy was transferred with his 210 Squadron to North Russia, for reconnaissance, and to provide cover for PQ 18 to Archangels. For several days he patrolled the Barentz Sea, taking part in the rescue of survivors from sunken ships with his Catalina P.

He was then asked to fly to Svalbard to fetch Captain Ernest Ullring and Ltn. Cmdr. R. A. Glen back to England. He started on 26th September, but halfway he met increasingly stormy weather and had to turn back. As he came out of the clouds about a hundred kilometres north of the Russian coast he was attacked by a FW 88. It came diving down to starboard, blazing away with its machine-guns, spraying bullets along the Catalina's fuselage, smashing the cockpit, and killing Healy. The FW 88 received several hits from the side-gunner on the Catalina at the back of its fuselage. The machine-gun in front jammed at the critical moment, and the German got away. The co-pilot took over, homing in on the Kildin Island and landing near the coast. They were picked by a Russian destroyer and brought to a naval station 2 hours away. Healy, the only member of the crew to be hit, was buried next day at a cemetery in the nearby village of Grasnaya, where other British servicemen were interred during the war.

According to reports Healy was probably suffering from fatigue after many long days patrolling the Barentz Sea. He did not take the usual avoiding action when the German pounced from behind, but held on his course. He was due for a long awaited rest on his return to England after his trip to Svalbard.

Only a month before, in August he had tried to fly to the North Pole in his Catalina P 210. He left Iceland and flew along the east coast of Greenland until 81° north when he developed engine trouble and had to turn back, flying practically on only one engine. He was met by a Norwegian Northrop sea-plane which escorted him back to Akureyri in Iceland.

At the summer station above Signehavn.

A "Catalina" outside Barentzburg.

Combined radio station, sickbay and commanding post after the attack, the author to the right.

In the mountains.
From the left: Hilmar Reksten, Ullring and the author.

After the attack. The radio hut with the gun Bofors II at the end of the coal heap.

The submarine "Seadog" back in Barentzburg.

Fox trapping and ptarmigan shooting. Ltn. Bowitz in the middle.

Baking bread in the ruins.

Sergeant Nore brought on board the destroyer "Onslaught".

Among the ships crew.

The American cruiser Tuscaloosa in Seydisfjord.

On the channel to Middelsburg.

British medical staff in Brussels.

Out from the pit, the author to the right.

Signehavn: the Attack on a German Meteorological Station

On 17th June Bredsdorff took over as governor of Svalbard. The same day, together with Ullring and eight others, I set off on a reconnaissance tour north along the west coast. Our task was to search for a German meteorological station, which had been located by radio and was assumed to be situated somewhere to the north round about Krossfjorden. In October 1942 a RAF plane had observed signs of what could have been human activity in Signehavn, and at the end of November Ullring had tried to make his way there on board the "Namsos", a Norwegian whaler borrowed from Iceland, where it did duty as a coastal patrol vessel; but blizzards and icing-up had made it impossible to reach Krossfjorden.

We set off in a 32-foot motor launch with a built-in cabin top forrard, equipped with a machine-gun and the usual small arms. We steered across the Isfjorden towards Alkhornet, a mountain to the north of the mouth of the fjord, where we went ashore, and searched the area, including Daumannen, a mountain a little further out. As we lay off the shore, a huge polar bear suddenly appeared, lumbering down further in towards the sea and swimming out. With its native curiosity it turned and made a bee-line for our boat. I immediately pulled out my film-camera, lay down on the cabin-top and started filming. All of a sudden an ear-piercing explosion rent the air to my immediate left, and at the same time I felt a stabbing pain in my ear. I nearly jumped out of my skin. A second-lieutenant, who should have known better, had taken a pot-shot at the bear, with the muzzle of his rifle close to my left ear. I told him in no uncertain terms just what I thought of his stupidity, but continued to film. When developed the film showed both sea and polar bear leaping into the air just as the shot went off. Another couple of rounds put paid to Master Bruin. We managed to drag the carcase to the water's edge, but had quite a job hauling it ashore. It was a he-bear, eight years old according to Ullring, with a fine coat, considering the time of year, and we succeeded in skinning and quartering it with the tools at our disposal. The bulk of the meat was stashed under a cairn of rocks for use as dog food, but we took two haunches with us, as these might help to supplement our rations. We also took the skin with us. Later on Ullring brought it with him to England.

The explosion had burst my left eardrum, and the other ear had also suffered, and for some time my hearing was somewhat impaired. It improved after a while, apart from certain permanent after-effects. Similar damage to an ear reduces one's ability to differentiate between sounds, making it difficult to distinguish one from another under noisy conditions, and consequently to apprehend speech in a babble of conversation.

The polar bear had delayed us on our journey north, and it was not until nine hours after leaving Barentsburg that we were able to set off again. We rounded Daumannsodden (Dead Man's Point), and steered a course through Forlandsundet, which runs for about 60 miles inside Prince Carl's Forland to the entrance of Krossfjorden.

Halfway up the sound we ran into fog. It was now late in the evening, as light as day, but poor visibility, and we considered it inadvisable to continue. All sea-marks—beacons and buoys—had been removed the year before, and ahead of us stretched the Forland reef, which runs right across the sound with numerous shallows and a depth of about a fathom, all the way from Murray Point on Forland to Sarstangen on the mainland. We spent part of the night ashore, under the open sky. It was bitterly cold and foggy, but I managed to snatch a few hours sleep.

We had also gone ashore because of the risk of being spotted by German "weather" planes, which were in the habit of coming over around 2 or 3 a.m., when it was advisable not to be caught in a boat off shore.

We had reached the bay in which Fridtjof Nansen had taken refuge on 12th July, 1912, when he was on an expedition to Svalbard in his 78-foot cutter "Veslemøy".

He had been lying weather-bound for several days in Grønnfjorden, off Finneset, where at that time there was a coal-mining community, as well as a whaling station and a telegraph station. When the weather improved he continued on his way north, but an area of intense low pressure moving in from the west, with increasing south-westerly winds, forced him to seek shelter once again, this time in Sandbukta at the southern end of Prince Carl's Forland. The wind increased in intensity, and he was soon compelled to take refuge in a new and better harbour, which he found in the bay to the north of Pool Point. Here he was safe. When the eye of the storm passed there was sunshine and a flat calm, but soon a fog descended, with increasing wind and blizzards from the north. Nansen knew what to expect, and promptly moved to the bay south of Pool Point where, 31 years later, we settled for the night.

For days on end Nansen endured strong icy winds from the north, with sleet and flurries of snow while he was here, in the month of July, before the storm finally abated. It took him as much as a week to reach Krossfjorden from Isfjorden.

This gives some idea of the sort of weather one can expect in Svalbard, especially on the west coast, where sunshine may give way to thick fog in next to no time.

One has heard tell of vessels from North Norway coming to Bear Island and Svalbard to catch seal, and of the crew of the longboats pulling for the shore in search of seal, while the parent ship lies further out; of fog suddenly reducing visibility making it impossible to find one's way back to the waiting ship. On occasion, too, if the fog persisted, the skipper, tired of waiting, would weigh anchor and sail back home. When the fog lifted the men in the longboat would find the vessel gone, and there would be nothing for it but to row back to Norway.

The cause of this sudden fog is that warm humid air from the Gulf Stream condenses on meeting the cold glaciers on the west coast and is then forced up.

When the fog lifted in the early hours of the morning, we continued on our way through Forlandsundet past the Forland Reef to Krossfjorden. Unlike Nansen we only spent a few hours on the trip.

At the mouth of Krossfjorden, on the right-hand side lies Kvadehuken, a flat extensive plain only just visible above the surface of the sea, and beyond it the ground rises steeply to another plain that stretches away inland. In common with Daumannsodden these are both typical of so many places on the coasts of Svalbard, where glacial action has ground down softer species of rock and levelled the landscape in different stages.

Kvadehuken had been mentioned as a possible site for a German meteorological station, but we never took this seriously, as the place is exposed to the sea, and is easily visible to passing ships.

On the left-hand side of the fjord entrance lies the Mitra Peninsula, with Mount Mitrafjell near its southern extremity, and Cape Mitra at its tip, on a wide flat stretch of land, just above sea-level.

Further in Krossfjorden runs north. On the left lies Ebeltofthamna, on the Mitra Peninsula, where the Germans maintained a meteorological station from 1910 and up to the first world war. There was now no sign of any such activity.

We continued east up Kongsfjorden, and the Kongsbre glacier with its broad steep ice-blue face now came into view, against a backdrop of peaks rearing up out of the mass of ice, at the head of the fjord. Countless ice-floes of all sizes came drifting down the fjord from the foot of the calving glacier. On the right lies the Brøgger Peninsula with Ny Aalesund halfway up the fjord, and immediately opposite Blomsterhalvøya (Flower Peninsula) jutting out from the northern shore.

We reached Ny Aalesund in the morning of 18th June. It was originally called King's Bay, after the coal-mining company that started operating there. It had its head office in the town of Aalesund on the west coast of Norway, which explains the change of name.

We landed at a derelict quay. Close by stood "Hotel Nordpol", its name in large letters on the facade and a general store on the ground floor. The houses were mere empty shells, and an eerie silence reigned: we had come to a ghost town. But the heaps of coal were still burning after the evacuation of 1941, when harbour installations and plant were destroyed. In one of the houses right at the back I found the doctor's surgery and the sick bay, where we proceeded to settle in. There was quite a lot of equipment left.

That evening we celebrated Ullring's 49th birthday. The bill of fare included polar-bear steak, beer and aquavit. We found the drinks in the cellar beneath the general store, and were surprised that the beer had survived two winters in a row.

The beer and aquavit were very welcome, but the steak was about the toughest meat I have ever eaten. What was more, it had a distinct taste of fish-oil.

A short distance to the south-east of the settlement stood the huge skeleton of the hangar that had been built prior to the flight of the airship "Norge" to the North Pole in 1926, and used two years later by the airship "Italia."

In those days New Aalesund was a hive of activity. On 21st May, 1925, Roald Amundsen, the first man to reach the South Pole, and Lincoln Ellsworth, American explorer, boarded two Dornier sea planes in an attempt to reach the North Pole, getting within 250 km of their goal before the attempt had to be abandoned when one of the planes developed engine failure.

In May 1926 Amundsen and the American, Richard Byrd*, were involved in a race to reach the Pole, the former in the airship "Norge" and the latter in a three-engine Fokker aeroplane "Josephine Ford". Byrd set off on 9th May with Floyd Bennet at the controls, flying to the Pole and back in $15\frac{1}{2}$ hours, and congratulated by his rival just before he

---

*There is some doubt as to whether Byrd reached the North Pole. Several publications argue that in view of the type of aeroplane which was used, its performance and the weight it carried, it would be unlikely that he reached the Pole during the time he was away, $15\frac{1}{2}$ hours, in spite of good weather condition. In addition there was an oil leakage of the right engine, and the notes which were made during the trip seemed to be somewhat unclear.

As it now also seems to be doubtful whether Peary reached the North Pole in 1909, then Ronald Amundsen could have been the first over both Poles together with Oscar Wisting.

in his turn set off. Amundsen crossed over the Pole and landed at Nome in Alaska, but his was a triumph with qualifications, as he had failed to reach the Pole first.

On 23rd May, 1928, it was Umberto Nobile's turn. In his airship the "Italia", the Italian general reached the Pole, but was unable to land, owing to dense fog, despite circling the spot for two hours. In the storm that followed his dirigible iced up, struck the ice and had its main gondola torn off, after which the airship rose sharply and vanished with six crewmen on board. The survivors stranded on the ice were later rescued. Amundsen volunteered to take part in the search, and on 18th June he took off in the seaplane Latham, never to return. I well remember the "Italia" on her way north to Svalbard, during a stop-off in Oslo, when the airship was moored to a mast at Lambertseter.

Amundsen was annoyed at failing to be the first to reach the North Pole, and in a way he had only himself to blame, as he had included in his team, in Svalbard Bernt Balchen, a skilled and keen pilot who could prove to be a great help. Balchen certainly proved helpful: he helped Byrd to make skis large enough for his plane; without them he would never have been able to take off.

When the airship "Norge" started, there was no room for Balchen, who had to be left behind, and watched her as she flew north. Byrd felt sorry for him and out of gratitude for his assistance and by way of consolation offered to include him in his crew. With Balchen on board Byrd's plane soon caught up with the "Norge", and flew alongside her for part of the way.

When the expedition was over Byrd took Balchen with him back to the USA, where he was employed as a test pilot for Fokker. In 1929 he accompanied Byrd on his expedition to the South Pole. After spending the winter in the "Little America" camp on the Ross Barrier, in November Balchen flew Byrd to the South Pole in a flight fraught with tense moments: he just managed to pilot the heavily laden aircraft through a gap in the mountains over two thousand metres high, and across the South Pole plateau after jettisoning several hundred kilos of provisions.

Early on the morning of 19th July we continued on our way up the Krossfjorden and entered Lilliehöökfjorden, one of the two arms of Krossfjorden which runs due north parallel to the coast and forms the Mitra Peninsula. At the head of the fjord the Lilliehöök Glacier, one of the largest glaciers in Svalbard, descends right down to the sea. The other branch of the fjord, the Møllerfjorden, cuts into the mountains to the east. Between them lies King Haakon's Peninsula.

As we moved up the fjord, more and more floes and blocks of ice came drifting down from the glacier, and at times we had to pole our way along. On some of the floes seal were lying, but they were so wary, that they disappeared into the water before we were within range. We soon had a clear and uninterrupted view of both sides of the fjord all the way to the glacier, but there was nothing special to be seen. However, the western shore was cleft by a bay with steep cliffs on both sides.

Hearts beat a little faster: if there was a meteorological station in this fjord, it would have to be situated in the bay, which opens up as we approach. All of a sudden a radio mast rears up, and a pair of huts comes into view behind a headland. Not a soul is to be seen.

We stepped ashore and approached the huts cautiously, with the finger on the trigger. No sign of life.

In the huts we found radio equipment, German uniforms, stores of provisions, and arctic gear. The aerial was a new, telescopic type, and was raised to half-mast. There was also an automatic weather-reporting station, a new invention.

The ground stretched, low and gently undulating, towards a number of small lakes. Further in it rose: to the south was a valley, but otherwise there were steep mountains on either side. The station had an abandoned air, and appeared not to have operated for some time.

We had arrived in Signehavn.

In 1906–1907 the arctic explorer Gunner Isachsen led an expedition to Svalbard sponsored by Prince Albert of Monaco. They spent some time in this bay, carrying out scientific work and charting the area. The bay was named after Isachsen's wife. The wide plain on the west of the peninsula, the Dieset Plain, was given the name of a lady botanist who accompanied the expedition. The Dieset valley runs up from the bay, and the Dieset lakes are situated on the plain which dominates the western part of the Mitra Peninsula and slopes up gradually toward the mountains in the eastern part of the peninsula.

Prince Albert of Monaco had sponsored an earlier expedition to Svalbard in 1898–1899, seizing the opportunity to have various geographical features named after himself, such as Mount Grimaldi in Krossfjorden, Grimaldi Bay in Forlandsundet, and Prince Albert's Mountain, to mention a few.

There was every probability that another station was to be found up in the mountains. We needed reinforcements and more equipment. Five men, under the command of a wireless operator, 2nd-Lieut. Augensen, were left behind. As there was no knowing how many Germans there were up in the hills, they were ordered to reconnoitre inland; a radio transmitter was left behind, as well as arms, ammunition and provisions.

After an interlude in Ny Aalesund we spent another night in Forlandsundet north of Dawes Point, so as not to be spotted by German planes. On the morning of the next day, 20th June, we were back in Barentsburg, where we were told that an alarming message had been received by radio from Signehavn. Another meteorological station had been discovered up in the hills. One of the Germans had shot himself, and five others had made their escape.

Next day we continued on our way north, this time in greater strength, with a Colt machine-gun mounted on deck as well as several automatic weapons, and ammunition and provisions for a month. Our boat had been hauled ashore to undergo various repairs owing to the buffeting she had received in the ice. Bredsdorff criticised Ullring for leaving troops to fend for themselves in the wilds. Originally he had not given permission for any foray beyond the other side of the fjord, as he considered our boat insufficiently armed and equipped to operate in foul waters, with the enemy in the air and under the surface, and with no sea-marks. But Ullring was not the man to let slip an opportunity of this kind: after all, there was a war on, and risks had to be taken.

There were now eleven of us: this time we had Hilmar Reksten with us. He had been to Longyearbyen, and got repairs and maintenance of the mines going. He had, after all, been one of the most ardent champions in favour of sending an expedition to Svalbard, as director of the mining company. We had a certain amount of rain and fog and poor visibility, and for this reason Ullring was at the helm for most of the time, as he had sailed this way the year before, and knew most of the headlands we passed: besides, owing to all the arms onboard, the compass was not entirely reliable, and had to be checked ashore before we set off across to the Kongs Fjord and past Kvadehuken.

Before noon next day we were at Signehavn. By now Lilliehöökfjorden was choked with drifting ice, and it took us nearly four hours to pole our way along. Calving from the glacier must have increased considerably during the last few days.

The men we had left behind had now settled down in one of the huts, and the radio transmitter was functioning well.

Two days before, on Sunday, 20th June, a German had strolled down to the camp, stripped to the waist in the sun and holding a small film camera. (We subsequently discovered that he was a keen zoologist by the name of Heinz Köhler who had been working as a nautical assistant.) When the guard saw him, the others were alerted, and hid themselves until he was quite close, whereupon they stepped forth and ordered him to put his hands up. He may not have understood the actual words, although their meaning should have been obvious. The man spun round and made off. A few warning shots were fired, and the men set off in pursuit, gradually overtaking him, until he suddenly stumbled. Pulling out a pistol he started firing wildly at his pursuers, at a range of twenty yards, without hitting anyone. When he realised that there was no escape, he turned his pistol on himself, and blew his brains out.

They realised that there must be other Germans in the area. Leaving one of their number behind on guard, the others continued on their way, up a steep slope. Further up the hill they came across a cluster of huts. They stormed it early in the morning of 21st June, only to find it deserted. The Germans must have left in a great hurry, but had time to remove the bolts from the machine-gun and small arms and pull down the aerial before they left. There were signs that five others had lived there. Our men immediately returned to the bay to report to Barentsburg.

In the evening of 20th June a Heinkel 111 had circled over the spot, which suggested that the Germans in Norway had been informed of the course of events. Next morning a Focke-Wulf Kondor with a bomb load arrived, and tried to make air-to-ground contact. Fortunately for us they were not certain whether their meteorologists had made their getaway, and dropped their bombs on the way back.

The German station up in the hills was put in order, and worked well with the German sets.

As soon as we had landed and been put in the picture, a small party of us set off inland to where the dead German lay. It was obvious that he had shot himself. There was a bullet wound in the right temple, and his head and the upper part of his body were daubed with blood.

In his report Franz Nusser, leader of the German expedition, alleges that we had shot him, and his report has served as a source for other versions of this episode; but the film I later took of the corpse refutes Nusser's contention.

For the time being we left the dead German where he lay and continued on our way to the station in the hills. The summer station, as it was called, was tactically well sited, concealed behind a number of hillocks but commanding a good view of Lilliehöökfjorden to the east. Beyond a ridge, there were also views to the west and the open sea, and south along the Dieset Plain in the direction of Mount Mitra, across the mouth of Krossfjorden all the way to Prince Carl's Foreland in the far distance.

The station contained several huts comprising living and sleeping quarters, a radio station and store hut, as well as meteorological instruments and an aerial outside. We found several parachute containers, and plenty of provisions and equipment. A great many personal effects had been left behind, including diaries from which it emerged that the German who had shot himself, Köhler, suffered from fits of depression. He had clearly found the long dark winter and the loneliness too much for him. Later on we learnt that friction had arisen between him and the others, in particular the leader of the expedition.

Köhler had also left behind a number of amateur paintings, primitive pictures of the surrounding scenery which Reksten took charge of. Before the war Köhler had apparently been a printer and painter, and had been recruited by the German navy's meteorological service to draw weather charts. He was also in charge of the radio-sonde ascents.

We reached the station in the afternoon of 22nd June, two days after it had been abandoned. Leaving four men behind on guard down by the bay, we settled into the huts. There were not many bunks, but we had no difficulty organising somewhere to sleep. The summer nights were light, and it was not particularly cold. In fact, even in our work it was hard to distinguish between night and day.

In the afternoon of the following day we sent out two patrols to look for the Germans, one west along the coast, the other, of which I was a member, south along the Dieset Plain.

We marched all night long across gently undulating country that presented no real obstacles. Here and there were patches of snow. After the spring thaw, the brooks, of which we had to cross a great many, were in spate.

There was still ice on the Dieset lakes. We found a boat, and later on an empty trapper's hut. We saw no sign of any Germans, but saw a few footprints. By midnight we were near Mount Mitra. We heard the rumble of artillery, but could see nothing out at sea. We decided to turn back.

We reached the summer station in the morning, after a trek of eleven hours, to receive a dramatic account.

After we had set off four men were left in the summer camp—Ullring, Reksten and a couple of others on look-out duty, and down by the bay four men were on guard duty. The two Ellefsen brothers, Petter and Einar together with Harald Andersen, were on board the motorboat, while Martiniussen was busy outside the wireless hut.

At 2300 hours Reksten discovers a U-boat gliding slowly towards the bay. He immediately alerts Ullring who joins him. Through their binoculars they watch the U-boat approaching the motorboat. Its silvery hull is difficult to spot in all the surrounding ice-floes. Ullring tries to contact the bay on the telephone, but gets no answer. All of a sudden the U-boat opens fire.

Ullring's immediate reaction is to run down and come to their aid, but Reksten advises against this, and Ullring reluctantly gives way. Shortly afterwards the motorboat starts to burn, before sinking. Shots are now fired from the U-boat at targets ashore, striking the rocks at the mountain camp, while the crew of the U-boat muster on deck. Are they preparing to land? All of a sudden the U-boat does a quick about-turn and disappears, after a bombardment lasting twenty minutes. This time, ignoring Reksten's warnings, Ullring sends Hans Breivik down to the bay.

After an hour two men emerge cautiously from behind a mound. They were Martiniussen and Petter Ellefsen. They imagined that the Germans were in the camp. Martiniussen told them that as soon as the shooting started he had rushed to the phone in the wireless hut, but failed to get through to the summer camp. Petter Ellefsen had been on duty in the motorboat; as soon as he spotted the U-boat, he alerted the two in the cabin, scrambled into the dinghy, and rowed for dear life to the shore, while the two men below donned life-jackets, jumped overboard and swam desperately for land while the bullets sprayed the water around them. Martiniussen had been lying ready behind a machine-gun, and had seen Andersen and Ellefsen scramble onto the ice, and try to drag themselves along the ground to find cover from the volley of shots. In doing this Andersen slipped back into the water and drowned. As long as the firing persisted it was impossible to come to their aid, as there was no available cover. Afterwards Andersen was dragged onto the ice, and given artificial respiration, but he had been in the water too long. Meanwhile Hans Breivik had arrived, and was giving a hand. Arne Ellefsen was exhausted and numb with cold; he was dressed in a German army greatcoat and taken up the hill, giving the men there quite a shock when they saw a man in a German uniform coming into view. He was taken good care of, given a change of dry clothes, placed in a warm bed, and given a couple of shots of brandy to thaw him out. The next day, when I returned to camp, he was in good shape.

I then made my way down to the bay and examined the corpse of Harald Andersen. There was no sign of any bullet wound, but clear symptoms of drowning.

Nusser's Report

Before the war Hans Knoespel had been a member of Herdemerten's expedition to West Greenland, and in 1941 he had been attached to the "Sachsen" floating weather-reporting station off the east coast of Greenland. He pointed out to the naval authorities the advantages of maintaining a permanent station in the Arctic during the winter. In his opinion for the winter of 1941–1942 the area round Krossfjorden in the north-west of Svalbard, would be highly suitable, while Signehavn was nicely concealed at the head of Lilliehöökfjorden. His plan was approved, and Operation "Knoespe" was organised.

At about the same time as the Luftwaffe established its station in the Adventdal at the beginning of October 1941, two ships, the "Homan" and the "Sachsen," left Kiel for Tromsø, proceeding via Bear Island, constantly alive to the danger of encountering enemy ships, and seeking cover whenever possible in the frequent fog banks, which without charts made navigation difficult. They were forced to rely on heaving the lead and the sound of breakers. They had no idea that Svalbard had been evacuated a month before and that there would therefore be little danger of being discovered.

They reached Signehavn on 15th October; this was a bay on the west side near the head of the Lilliehöök Fjord. Patrols were sent out to reconnoitre. After 2 weeks the station had been set up in two huts, and transmission started. Tours of inspection were carried out around Krossfjorden, along the coast, and on 15th November the two ships left after dynamiting their way through the ice.

During the three months when the sun never shone they continued sending weather reports to Norway, but in February, with the return of the sun, Knoespe was afraid they might be discovered; for this reason they built a summer station higher up in the hills, where there were good views to the south, and the entrance to Krossfjorden could be kept under surveillance, while radio conditions were better. Two reserve depots were also set up, and extra supplies were dropped from the air.

When the Norwegians arrived at Barentsburg in May 1942, the Germans no longer felt secure, and discontinued transmission, so as not to be detected. Evacuation was now on the cards, but not till 23rd August did a U-boat arrive to pick them up. Equipment was left behind, the station in the hills dismantled and stored there, and an automatic transmitter was installed working on batteries that lasted a few months.

To avoid detection the U-boat returned to Norway by sailing to the northward of Svalbard, through waters which as a rule are choked with drifting ice in summer and difficult to negotiate; but conditions that year were good, and they were only forced to submerge once. Proceeding on a course through the Hinlopen Straits they reached Narvik without further incident.

Even before Knoespel was back, plans were being laid for the next expedition to Signehavn for the winter of 1942–1943. It was code-named "Nussbaum" after its leader, the Austrian polar explorer Franz Nusser, who had visited Svalbard before the war, and was now busily engaged in the work of preparation. The idea was to transport the expedition by boat. However, in the meantime a Norwegian garrison had arrived in Svalbard, and there was the risk of being discovered, and even that the station might already have been detected. But as conditions were so favourable, it was decided that the risk was worth taking, although some alteration in the plan would have to be made: they would have to go by U-boat, and only equipment that would go through the hatch in the conning-tower could be included. Some of this was sent by sea to the U-boat base in Narvik, and some by train through Sweden. Nusser and Knoespel, who would put him in the picture with regard to Signehavn, also travelled by train through Sweden to Narvik, together with a few other members of the expedition.

On 12th October U-Boat 277 slipped out of the basin in Narvik, and made her way to Signehavn, where the ice had already started to settle. Returning immediately to Narvik, the U-boat came back to Svalbard, this time with the remaining members of the expedition and their equipment, where she hove to at the edge of the ice in the bay, enabling unloading to proceed rapidly and smoothly on sledges across the ice. Although the ice threatened to close around the U-boat, she broke loose and returned to Norway with Knoespel on board.

Among the items of equipment they had been unable to bring with them were hydrogen containers, to be used with the radio-sonde ascents.

However, the Germans were now producing hydrogen by means of a chemical process, by infusing sodium hydroxide on aluminium bits, a new invention. This is a highly corrosive fluid, and it was considered unduly risky to transport large quantities in the narrow confines of a U-boat. Furthermore large amounts of water were required for its production, and this was hard to come by in Signehavn in winter. As a result of all these problems the use of radio-sondes had to be discontinued already in January.

Radio-sondes are sent aloft with the aid of small balloons filled with hydrogen. They contain instruments that measure air pressure, temperature and humidity in the upper atmosphere, and a radio transmitter conveys the readings to the ground. They can attain an altitude of 30,000 metres before the balloon bursts and the instruments float down to earth on the end of a small parachute.

Owing to the presence of intervening mountains, wireless contact between Signehavn and Tromsø in North Norway was poor. As winter drew to a close a summer station was set up in the hills, and this provided good contact. The Germans put in a great deal of hard work carrying up equipment and building material in the dark and the cold, often through deep snow.

Provisioning by air involved just as big problems. If there was fog or poor visibility, planes were unable to drop their containers, and if the weather in Svalbard was good, then as a rule it was bad in Norway. The first drop was supposed to be carried out in the beginning of March, but the first successful one occurred early in May; a fresh drop took place two weeks later. The planes used were Focke-Wulf 200 Kondors.

Nusser reports that they lived in constant fear of an attack by the Norwegian garrison in Barentsburg. As there was also the danger of being "fixed" by radio location, they dared not start transmitting to Tromsø before Lilliehöökfjorden had been frozen over at the end of November. Not till then would they feel secure from any undesirable visit.

The summer station was also sited up in the hills for security reasons, as it enjoyed fine views as far as the sea to the west and the entrance to Krossfjorden, besides, it was easier to reach the reserve camp, in the event of an attack on Signehavn. The reserve camp was situated on Mount Lundtvedt, to the west of the summer camp.

On 20th June, 1943, Nusser made his way down to the winter camp together with his wireless operator Ehrich and his nautical assistant Garbarty. He had been ordered to check the stores, and was also out to shoot a seal or two so as to obtain fresh meat.

Standing by the water's edge, and scanning the ice-floes for signs of seal, they suddenly see an armed man emerging from one of the huts. Without being observed, they withdraw cautiously back up the hill. Not only have they no idea of the numerical strength of the enemy, but they themselves are armed only with a hunting rifle and a shotgun.

Ehrich is sent back to the summer camp to inform the others, and send a message to Tromsø, while Nusser and Garbarty stay behind to cover him.

When they estimated that he had got there, Garbarty followed, with orders to organise defensive posts, while Nusser remained behind to watch developments. After a while, having seen no one else, he withdrew.

The Germans were at a loss to explain how the enemy had reached the bay, as they had seen no boat of any kind arrive, and concluded that they had landed in Seal Bay, which lies a little further down the fjord and was not visible from the summer camp.

When Nusser arrived he was told that Köhler had gone off down to Diesetdalen to film the bird life on some of the lakes. Shortly afterwards they had heard shooting from down below, and the men on duty reported that they had seen Köhler, stripped to the waist, running away from four men who were firing at him. The last they saw of him was when he was taking cover behind some boulders, constantly under fire.

Nusser states that Köhler was unarmed, and had been shot by his pursuers. He cannot have known that Köhler carried a pistol. Köhler's death brought about the demise of Harald Andersen.

Nusser now realised that there were patrols looking for them up Diesetdalen, and they would soon be tracked down, and for this reason it was a matter of urgency to transfer to the reserve camp. Operation "Nussbaum" was now pointless, as repeated attacks would make it impossible to operate the station, which consisted of only five men. For this reason "Gruppe Nord" in Norway was informed of the withdrawal to the reserve camp, KRA, and asked to dispatch a U-boat to evacuate the party.

It was important to make a quick getaway, taking with them only the most important items, and refraining from setting fire to the station, as this would reveal their whereabouts.

The route to the reserve camp lay across the Dronning Glacier, which runs from the massif at the upper end, down between Queen Maud's Mountain and Mount Natrud, in the direction of the Dieset plain. The camp was admirably sited, with good views of the sea to the west and across the western end of the Dieset plain to Krossfjorden in the south. At the same time it was well protected from the east, and was abundantly supplied with provisions and equipment.

That very evening German planes were over, and next day they tried to drop containers, but these fell in the sea. Reconnaissance of the summer camp had shown that it was occupied by the enemy. On the night of 22nd June a U-boat approached the coast at speed, making straight for the agreed rendez-vous. Nusser and his men had hurriedly packed their gear and set off down to the coast. After a while the U-boat headed back to the open sea: it had taken the men on the run too long to reach the coast. The thaw had produced a great many swollen brooks which had to be negotiated. When they finally got down, there was no sign of the U-boat. They dared not linger on the beach, where they risked being discovered, while the reserve camp was too far away, should the U-boat return. In the event they set up camp at the southern end of Mount Natrud, where there was good cover from the east, and uninterrupted views north as far as the moraine fronting the southern-most of the seven glaciers. Provisions were fetched from the other camp.

The weather had been bitterly cold, with showers of rain, and now fog rolled in from the sea. At four in the morning gunfire out at sea could be heard, and shortly afterwards the shape of a U-boat loomed up, gliding south along the coast.

Nusser's men fired a flare, and in reply the U-boat ran up a yellow flag. As they had received no instructions regarding this recognition signal, they were uncertain of the boat's identity, and not till the German naval ensign had been run up did they fire another flare, whereupon the U-boat hove to, and lowered a dinghy in which Nusser and his men were brought aboard.

The crew of the U-boat had seen no signs of them when it first approached the coast. For this reason it had proceeded north to the terminal moraine of the first of the glaciers strung out along the coast, as there was a trapper's hut there, which during the planning of the expedition had been singled out as a potential retreat. Sailing past in dense fog the crew of the U-boat had fired four shots as a recognition signal; but there was no sign of life on land, and the boat had turned about and once again proceeded south.

With Nusser and his men safe on board, they now sailed north to Magdalenafjorden where they stayed till evening, after which the Germans turned south into Krossfjorden to take a look at Ny Aalesund, where there was no sign of life, and then proceeded north into Lilliehöökfjorden. Near Signehavn the diesel engines were stopped, and the electric propulsion unit switched on. Catching sight of our motorboat, they approached slowly. When 60 yards off, the U-boat was spotted by the soldier on duty, who raised the alarm. The U-boat opened fire, and the motorboat was sunk by three well-aimed shots, and the huts on land were raked by bullets. The U-boat then withdrew, and on 28th June reached Narvik. So much for Nusser's report.

When the motorboat went down our radio transmitter went with it. We were now completely cut off from the outside world. However, the very next day one of our wireless operators, Augensen, managed to fix the German transmitter, and a message was sent to Barentsburg describing what had happened; contact was made with the UK, and on Sunday, 27th June we were told that a submarine would be coming from the Shetlands to fetch us on 1st July. Not surprisingly our spirits, which during the last few days had been at a low ebb, rose considerably.

On 25th June I made my way down to the bay and examined the body of Köhler. Apart from the bullet wound and blood there was no other sign of a wound. He was buried close by the spot, and we placed a cross over his grave, inscribed with his name and the date. The next day Harald Andersen was buried near the shore with full military honours. It was a solemn occasion, with Ullring conducting the service and a salvo fired over the grave. A cross was raised on the grave which was adorned with Arctic flowers.

Ullring had been greatly depressed by the incident, blaming himself for the death of one of his men, and for a time kept very much to himself. While I was away on the reconnaissance tour down the Mitra Peninsula a message was received to the effect that the British had intercepted a signal from a German U-boat that it was apparently on its way to Signehavn to avenge the death of Köhler. At the time I knew nothing of this, but Ullring has subsequently confirmed it. He had told the men stationed in the bay what to expect.

His plan was that, as soon as the U-boat appeared, its deck would be raked with fire from the men in the motorboat, thus preventing the German crew from manning the gun.

The moment Ullring, from his post up the hill, heard the shots fired by the U-boat's gun, he knew his plan had failed. Petter Ellefsen, who was on duty, spotted the U-boat all of a sudden at a distance of 60 yards. He thought he saw a second U-boat, and didn't open fire. Reksten, too, admits that at first he imagined he saw two U-boats, but it must have been a large block of ice in the water which resembled the silvery white camouflaged hull.

Ullring's plan was bold but not entirely realistic. If the U-boat had surfaced closer, it might have been possible to carry out the plan. But it had approached stealthily, gliding along among the ice floes with its engines switched off and ready to fire. Ellesfsen did not stand a chance. Later on we successfully dealt with a U-boat that turned up off Barentsburg, when by firing our anti-aircraft gun we prevented its crew from manning the cannon.

If our defence had been based on shore, and our boat had been lying close to the beach, our chances of defending ourselves would have been better, and we should not have lost our motorboat. If we had all been assembled in the hill station, lives would have been saved; the German U-boat crew would never have despatched a task force up the hill to attack us in our favourable defensive position, not knowing how many men we could muster. They were not prepared for that kind of operation: they would have to count on losing several of their number, with very little to show for it, as the station would be useless once it had been discovered; but we should perhaps have lost our motorboat. The chief aim of the Germans was probably to isolate us; but if the Germans could be rescued, so could we.

It is probable that Reksten influenced Ullring's tactics, as he also appeared to have done later on, it was safer in the mountains to keep a guard down in the bay, and possibly save the boat, even though there was a risk of someone being killed.

The intercepted message from the U-boat apparently indicated that the meteorological team had been taken onboard, but Ullring had undoubtedly not been told of this, even if he assumed that this was probably the case. On 29th June he had in fact suggested that we should carry out a reconnaissance northward to the Lilliehöök Glacier. I accompanied Ullring on this trip. We were both armed with pistols, and I also carried a rifle. Moving around unarmed in the wilds of Svalbard is not to be recommended. The enemy was one thing, meeting a polar bear was another; these creatures are always aggressive, and at their most dangerous when the pangs of hunger gnaw. At times when there has been little drifting ice and seals have been hard to catch, a polar bear may go for long periods without food. Seals are his most important source of food, and a seal lying on an ice-flow can more easily be surprised by a bear swimming.

We reached the glacier and climbed as far as the Forbes Glacier, a branch of it that runs west. Here we searched behind some projecting rocks, but could find no trace of life or human activity. The lateral glacier we were on runs all the way to the ice-massif above, where it joins the Lillihöök Glacier further north. From this tributaries run west, gracing the coastal landscape with seven glaciers, all in a row, to the north in the direction of Magdalenafjorden.

We realised there was little point in continuing up the Lilliehöök Glacier: no one would ever dream of escaping that way, as this would involve a 20-kilometre slog all the way to the head of the Smeerenburg Fjord. Without adequate preparation and special equipment it would be a perilous and crazy undertaking in a frozen wilderness with treacherous crevasses presenting an extra hazard.

It was strange to consider that more than three hundred years ago as many as a thousand Dutchmen had been engaged in whaling in these bleak regions of the Arctic. Every summer a town of some thousand souls would spring up on Amsterdam Island. Close by, across the Danish Sound at Virgo Harbour, the Swede Andrée many years later had made the first attempt to reach the North Pole by balloon. This was in 1897. The balloon was blown east, and its crew of three, Andrée, Strindberg and Fränkel, perished near Kvitøya.

When we returned to the summer camp we learned that two of our men had discovered the German reserve camp; it contained little equipment, and we were pretty sure that they had made their getaway in the U-boat.

We were soon busily engaged preparing for the arrival of our submarine; vital equipment had to be brought from the summer camp down to the bay, but only the most essential could be accommodated in the sub. Before leaving the camp in the morning of 1st July, we set fire to all the huts, including equipment and provisions, while the installations outside were destroyed. Flames from the burning huts shot high into the air, while exploding flares and tracer ammunition provided a veritable Brock's benefit firework display. Down by the bay the aerial was taken to pieces: Ullring thought it might be of interest to the British. Other essential radio equipment was carried down to the shore.

A long and restless period of waiting ensued, and some of our party were clearly on edge. Would the submarine arrive?

At last, at one o'clock it appeared round the point, and hove to a short distance off shore. Our task was now to embark personnel and gear as quickly as possible, as the sub presented a sitting target to enemy aircraft. We rowed like men possessed, weaving our way round floes and blocks of ice until we were pretty exhausted. Our major problem was how to get the aerial out to the sub and down the conning-tower hatch. Finally, at 0300 GMT we set off down the fjord, and the station disappeared astern in a flurry of fire and smoke from the burning huts.

We proceeded on the surface south down Lilliehöökfjorden, but when we reached Krossfjorden a German plane was observed flying north. In a trice we were clear to submerge. All hands below deck, hatches closed. Switch off diesel engines, dynamos humming low. In the confined space of the wardroom we listened intently. Had we been spotted?

Nothing happened, and after a while we surfaced cautiously. There was no sign of any plane. But near Forlandsundet the plane reappeared flying south, and once again we had to submerge, after which we were able to continue on the surface as far as Barentsburg, where we arrived at 1500 hours GMT. The German plane had been observed here too.

The submarine, HMS "Seadog," remained here until the following day, 3rd July. The evening before we had enjoyed a convivial party in the wardroom, but in the morning yet another German plane was sighted, and the crew of the sub were in a hurry to get away.

The Germans had now been deprived of their weather-reporting service in Svalbard, apart from a few automatic stations; these were not sufficient for their needs, and they now worked feverishly to find a replacement, finally settling for a station in Liefdefjorden in North

Svalbard, to the north-east of Lilliehöökfjorden. This operated during the winter of 1943–44.

Code-named "Kreuzritter," the expedition was led by Knoespel, and consisted of twelve men in all. Our action in Signehavn had compelled the Germans to take measures for military protection. The expedition left Hammerfest on board the trawler "K. J. Busch," escorted by U-boat 355, on 4th October. Two days later the mouth of Liefdefjorden was reached, and a reserve depot was established at Reinsdyrflya. The station was set up opposite Sørdalsbukta a little further in, and a reserve camp beyond the hill at the head of Raudefjorden. With the aid of the U-boat all surrounding fjords were reconnoitred, including Signehavn, where the depots were found to be untouched.

On 1st December the fjord was frozen over, and transmission was immediately started, continuing until as late as 1st June. In April 1944 three men were dispatched to the camp in Raudefjorden in order to carry out comparable transmissions, and to keep watch on the coast. A guard was also placed on the Reinsdyrflya depot. In May supplies were dropped from the air.

A few hours before a U-boat was due to evacuate the party on 30th June, Knoespel went to detonate a mine that had been placed as a booby-trap in a trapper's hut in the event of an enemy patrol arriving. This was now due to be immobilised to ensure that no trapper in the future would be killed, but in detonating the mine Knoespel was killed. Before leaving the Germans left an automatic met. station on Sørdalsflya.

That same winter of 1943–44 an expedition,code-named "Schatz-gräber," was sent to Franz Josef Land under Walter Dress, with Alfred Makus as military commander and Georg Hoffmann as medical officer. They left Kiel onboard the "Kehdingen," commanded by Captain Hartmann. Their departure was delayed when the expedition's equipment, lying on the quay, was destroyed in a bombing attack on the town. They sailed in convoy to Tromsø, where they were joined by a gyro-equipped U-boat.

Ice conditions were good, and drifting ice was not encountered until they were 50 nautical miles south of the archipelago which was Soviet territory. On 8th September they landed at Cambridge Bay on the south side of Alexander Island, the westernmost of the islands situated about 80° North Latt. and 45° East Long. As there wasn't much snow they were forced to carry all the equipment up to the hut which they erected some way from the beach. After a week the "Kehdingen" and its U-boat escort departed, and they set about making preparations for winter. They found ample supplies of driftwood, which came in handy for fuel in addition to the coal they had brought with them. The hut was constructed with double walls, and its various rooms were roofed over with additional tarpaulins. Extra protection, insulation and camouflage were also provided by the snow, but they were compelled to keep their stoves burning round the clock. In October, with the temperature 15° below zero, the bay froze over, and on 1st November they were able to start transmitting.

A reserve depot had been set up, and when the light returned in February another was established on the north coast. In May supplies were dropped from the air, with planes homing in on a radio beacon, as strong winds made navigation difficult.

In order to vary their monotonous fare, they shot a polar bear, relishing the juicy meat. Shortly afterwards, however, one by one fell victim to high temperatures and violent stomach pains. Soon they were all confined to bed, apart from the medical officer, who had eaten more sparingly of the meat, which had been contaminated with trichinae, and who was in a position to nurse his companions. By contacting a doctor in Oslo, they managed to receive radioed instructions on precautions to be taken and treatment, and it was decided to evacuate the party for hospitalisation, though this proved somewhat of a problem, as it was May, and the ice was breaking up, making it difficult for planes to land. An airstrip was therefore dynamited on land; and a FW 200 tried to touch down, but skidded off the makeshift runway and lost a wheel. A plane, carrying a spare wheel, flew all the way up from Marseille, to effect the necessary repairs. The entire party managed to squeeze on board, after leaving all their equipment behind. Thanks to a favourable wind they just managed to take off and fly to Banak in North Norway. From here they continued to a hospital in Oslo. Later on a U-boat was dispatched to fetch their equipment.

In the autumn of 1944 the Germans chose Nordaustlandet in Svalbard as a site for a new met. station. It was well out of the range of Allied operations, and difficult of access; it also made less demand on the Navy, which was hard pressed to provide vessels at a time when Germany was in dire straits. There was game in abundance, and driftwood from Siberia provided ample fuel. The leader of the expedition, code-named "Haudegen," was Wilhelm Dege, who had been a member of several pre-war expeditions to Svalbard. The trawler "H. J. Bush" was waiting in Narvik to embark a party of eleven. The U 357, detailed as escort, and carrying some of the supplies and equipment, was unexpectedly ordered to proceed immediately to the waters off Björnöya (Bear Island) in order to take part in an attack on a Murmansk convoy. She was lost, and with her the equipment intended for use by the expedition. The U 507 was assigned as a replacement. A patrol in the vicinity of Svalbard had reported the presence of two Allied aircraft carriers and eight destroyers.

It was therefore decided to proceed through the Hinlopen Strait after it had been established that the waters were free of ice and enemy forces.

They left Hammerfest on 10th September, and reached the Rijp Fjord three days later. Next day they made their way to the head of the fjord at Wordie Bay, situated at 80° N. Lat., where a hut was erected. Here they were safe from enemy attack, as the fjord was ice-bound for most of the year and as a rule only navigable in July. It was also within easy reach, should a retreat be necessary, of the head of the Wahlenberg Fjord where the U-boat had left a reserve depot.

The possibility of a local ridge of high pressure over the glaciers capable of influencing meteorological observations, had been taken into account, although this had not been established by the 1935–36 Oxford University expedition.

The U-boat made a detour round Nordaustlandet, carrying out scientific observations and setting up two additional reserve depots at the head of the Duve Fjord and Albertine Bay further east on the north coast.

The limit of drift ice was comparatively far north, but from time to time large icebergs would come drifting down through the Hinlopen Strait. On 27th September the trawler and the U-boat returned to Narvik, and on 18th October the sun was visible for the last time. It would not reappear until the following 1st March. By the end of November everything was set for starting the transmission of meteorological observations. Unlike a great many other expeditions the winter passed pleasantly enough with working routine and various forms of entertainment. With the arrival of spring a number of defensive measures were undertaken to forestall enemy attack. However, on 7th May came the news of Germany's capitulation and they were now able to devote themselves entirely to scientific work, as well as excursions to surrounding fjords and glaciers.

Orders were received to make ready for evacuation on 7th August, but no boat arrived, and with the onset of stormy weather and blizzards they made preparations for spending another winter in Svalbard. Finally, at the end of the month, Dege was asked to report on ice conditions. As these were favourable the Norwegian seal catcher "Blaasel" was despatched, arriving on 3rd September. The party surrendered to Skipper L. Albertsen. Three days later they left, with all their equipment on board, on a course to the east of Nordaustlandet, landing on 13th September in Tromsø, where they were interned.

Not only did German weather planes carry out daily reconnaissance flights north along the west coast of Svalbard, but similar operations were undertaken further east over Soviet territory. In July 1942 Schütze had landed on Meshduscharskij, an island west of Novaya Semlya, to investigate the possibility of installing an automatic transmitter. Unfortunately his plane got bogged down in the marshy ground, and he was forced to have planks and tools flown up from Banak in order to take off. He had landed without permission, and expected to be severely reprimanded on his return; but thanks to his enterprise and good luck he was let off lightly.

The Germans were determined to try again, when the ground would be frozen. Accordingly on 13th October, Schütze and his crew took off in a Heinkel 111. Retaining full power, he tested the surface with his landing wheels; the ice appeared to be firm and he now decided to make a landing. All went well until the aircraft came to a halt, when the undercarriage broke through the ice, a repeat of last time's performance. But this time they had the necessary equipment, and made hasty preparations for take-off, while unloading the automatic transmitter "Kröte." Busily involved in this work, they suddenly spot a Soviet flying-boat to the north, which has clearly observed them and now approaches. They take cover as the Russian plane circles the spot before making off to the north. A little later it returns, and continues to circle, firing its machine guns but without recording a direct hit. Striving desperately to extricate their plane from the marsh, the German crew enjoy a temporary respite when a Ju 88 appears on the horizon, and chases the Russian away. Half-an-hour later the Ju 88 abandons the scene and once again the Russians return and open fire, but with no more success than before. By now it is getting dark. As they had been discovered they were now forced to dismantle the transmitter and take it back with them, as this was a new invention that ought not to fall into enemy hands. The aerial and batteries, however, were left behind. It was now quite dark, and the Russian flying-boat had withdrawn. Giving full throttle the pilot managed, thanks to the provisional plant runway, to get airborne. Shortly afterwards they landed at Banak. Subsequent reconnaissance flights showed that the Russians had examined the contents of the abandoned crates.

When in 1943 the "Luftwaffe" tried to find a new location for a meteorological station after having lost Signehavn, Schütze searched over Bjørnøya and found a possible landing ground in the northwest part of the island in the middle of October. When he tried to land, he suddenly found himself rushing into rocky ground which had not been visible from the air. Only by a quick pull on the stick was he able to save himself from going headlong into disaster. However, as the place was considered suitable for the purpose it was decided to go ahead, and 4 men were parachuted down. They managed to land between the rocks without any bones broken. They cleared a 500 metre long narrow strip, so narrow that when Schütze landed with a party of nine men only his skill saved the tips of the wings from damage. The men helped to enlarge the runway and then set off on a reconaissance search for possible enemy troops. They found the weather station had been robbed of anything of importance by the British the year before when they stopped on their way back from Svalbard. All radio equipment had been removed.

The weather conditions on Bjørnøya were very bad, with much fog, frequent storms and blizzards which made it difficult to land. At last at the end of October they managed to set up an automatic weather station. It worked for only 2 weeks and the whole project was abandoned. They had more success with the one they set up in August 1942 with a runway on Sydkappøya, the south point of Svalbard.

In 1943 the Arado Airplane factory had produced a Caterpillar-airplane with 10 pairs of wheels which could land on the tundra. On snow runners could be fixed under the wheels. Schütze went to Germany to have a look and flew it back to Banak. With this plane they established an automatic transmitter on Bjørnøya and Sydkappøya. A manned station was set up on the southeast coast of Edgeøya at Dianadalen. The Island lies southeast of Svalbard.

By the time the station on Bjørnøya had been set up the runway had become somewhat soft and the wheels on one side of the new plane dug in and got stuck. As on Novaya Semlja they had to have planks and tools brought up to become airborne.

One drawback with this plane AR 232 A, was that if one engine cut out the other one could not keep the plane airborne. Schütze was therefore to fly it back to Germany to have the problem dealt with. On 26th August he started from Banak with a full crew and 20 ratings going home on leave. The weather was bad with low clouds. When they failed to turn up at Værnes Airfield near Trondheim a search was started. The aircraft had crashed in the mountains north of Banak and all on board were killed. The cause of the disaster was supposed to be exactly the fault it was going back to Germany to have repaired, that one engine had cut out.

In spite of the weather station the Airforce set up on Bjøornøya, the German Navy had in 1943 set up four automatic stations of their own on the northcoast of the island. Another sign of the bad co-operation between the two services.

On the 30 km long and narrow island Hopen about 200 km southeast of Svalbard the Germans had meteorological stations with 4 men during both the winters 1943–44 and 1944–45. Beforehand they had attended a special training camp for arctic personnel at Finse near the Hardangjøkul. It had also been attended by some Norwegian volunteers who later worked on Bear Island and South Cape. On Hopen it had both times proved difficult to land from a U-boat, and a great part of the

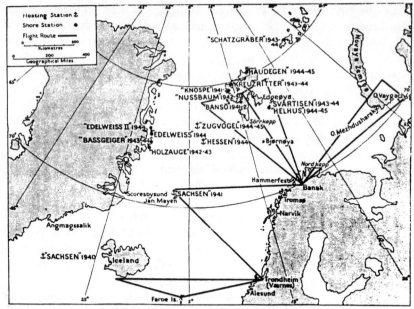

Map to illustrate German meteorological activities in the Arctic, 1940–45.

equipment got lost in the strong surf, as was the case with the building material. They had therefore to spend the winter in a trapper's hut, on the southeast coast of the island. The same hut had been used by 4 survivors from a torpedoed Russian ship, who spent the winter there from November 1942, until they were picked up by a German U-boat in the spring and brought to Kirkenes. Later 20 skeletons were found on the shore.

For safety reasons the transmission was not started before the island was shut in by the ice in November. It lasted until June when the ice was breaking up. The last expedition was fetched in August 1945 by the Norwegian ship "Skandfer", brought to Svalbard and then to Tromsø. During the winter they had also shot a polarbear to vary on the food. But they were wise enough to have the meat microscoped for trichinae before eating it.

The Germans also made use of a number of floating met. stations in northern waters. Some of these were anchored to the ocean floor, and were so designed that they surfaced every time they were due to make recordings and transmit, but otherwise remained submerged. They were placed in position by U-boats, some as far from home waters as the coast of Labrador.

At the end of October 1944 the "Zugvogel" expedition consisting of four men, was despatched on board the "Wuppertal" in order to obtain weather reports from the ice barrier between Svalbard and East Greenland. She was under the command of Adolf Schönfeld, and had a crew of 17. At the end of January she sent her last report, a warning of increasing gales, and was never heard of again.

The war in Svalbard was a war for weather reports; meteorological observations transmitted from the Arctic were vital to the conduct of the campaign. Inevitably this led to a struggle for a monopoly on weather reports also from Greenland.

Greenland

After the occupation of Denmark in 1940 Greenland remained in a vacuum; the only link with the "Mother Country" was by radio, and any news received from Copenhagen was German-inspired. The governor, Eske Brun, assumed that the King and the Government were opposed to the idea of Greenland being ruled by the Germans. He was responsible for the world's largest island, with a population of 22 thousand souls, with no means of defence. Faced with this dilemma he contacted the USA through the Danish Minister in Washington, Henrik Kaufmann, and it was agreed that Greenland would be given the status of a temporary American protectorate. The USA realised that in the long run they were bound to be involved in the war, and for this reason it was important to secure bases in Greenland. On 7th June, 1941, President Roosevelt sanctioned a plan for the defence of Greenland, and in the same year, the first American airforce base and met. station were set up on the south-west coast near Julianehaab, the first of several others. These proved of vital importance to the Atlantic convoy service, especially in conjunction with the Danish and Norwegian weather-reporting stations on the east coast of Greenland as well as in Iceland, Jan Mayen and Svalbard.

Greenland was discovered by Eric the Red (Eirik Raude) in 982 after he had been outlawed from Norway and her Icelandic colony, and settled in the area now occupied by Julianehaab. His son Leiv Erikson discovered North America in the year 1000, when he came to Newfoundland, which he called Vinland, built a house and spent the winter there.

Norse settlement gradually spread north up the west coast of Greenland, while at the same time native Eskimos moved south. For some mysterious reason the population on the west coast died out some time in the 14th century, at about the same time as the Black Death ravaged Norway, and Greenland was now ruled from Copenhagen. A fresh wave of colonisation started after the missionary Hans Egede arrived in 1721. When Norway severed her links with Denmark in 1814, the latter retained Greenland, but Norwegians regarded East Greenland as no-man's land, and continued hunting, trapping and fishing. In 1931 Norway annexed part of the east coast around Myggbukta and when Denmark lodged a protest with the International Court in the Hague, she was in 1933 awarded sovereignty of the whole of Greenland.

Geologically the ground beneath the vast inland ice-cap has been pressed down like a dish as much as several hundred metres below sea level.

When the weather reporting stations in the autumn of 1940 started transmitting in code, in order to deprive the Germans of the information they contained, the latter were forced to establish their own stations, and it was imperative for the allies to prevent this.

In order to monitor any German landing on the east coast, the Danish Sledge Patrol was set up under the command of Ib Poulsen, with its headquarter at Eskimones. One of its member was the Norwegian Henry Rudi, the legendary arctic bear-hunter, who had mainly hunted in Svalbard. Danish members of the patrol included Marius Jensen and Kurt Olsen as well as a number of Eskimos. The latter had no conception of war, and could not grasp the idea of fighting against other human beings, and for this reason they were never sent out on patrol except in the company of others in the event of an encounter with the enemy. They were mainly used as dog-team drivers, at which they were past masters. Off the coast the Greenland Naval Patrol was established, consisting of the ice breaker "Northland" and two other US Coast Guard vessels, under the command of Rear-Admiral E. H. Smith.

In September 1940 the Germans attempted to establish a meteorological station on the east coast using the sealing vessel "Buskö", which had a Norwegian crew, under the command of the trapper Halvard Devold, who in 1931 had raised the Norwegian flag, in Myggbukta and occupied part of the surrounding country. The "Buskö" was seized, the crew members who had been landed with radio equipment were quickly tracked down, and all the members of the expedition were sent to the USA.

In March 1943, when the sun returned and weather conditions improved, a patrol set off from Eskimones for Sabine Island, some 100 kilometres to the north, consisting of Marius Jensen and two Eskimos, each with a sledge and a dog-team of about 10 huskies.

They reached the Sandodden trapping station on the south side of Wollaston Foreland and continued north on the difficult route round the coast with its hummocks and open channels.

After some hard going they could see Germaniahavn, a considerable distance away on the south side of Sabine Island, where there was a

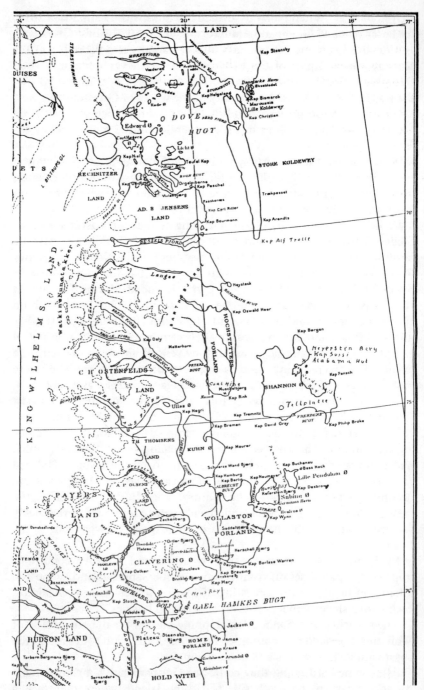

The East Coast of Greenland

trapper's hut. At this point the dogs pricked up their ears; using their binoculars the men observed smoke rising from the chimney, and shortly afterwards two figures were seen to emerge, making their way up the slope and disappearing over the brow.

In a state of complete exhaustion the members of the patrol entered a warm hut, with a blazing fire and coffee cups on the table still containing warm coffee, and found a green tunic with the swastika on the breast. Obviously the enemy was not far away and was bound to return soon. With no means of defending themselves, the patrol would have to make its way back to Eskimones as quickly as possible and report. Jensen had his work cut out persuading the Eskimos and the dog-teams, exhausted as they were, to set off on the long trail back. In the end they made their way back across the fjord to a trapper's hut at Cape Wynn, where they spent the night. Jensen had not really understood the danger involved.

On 22nd August, 1942, the German trawler "Sachsen" had left Tromsø with the members of the "Holzauge" expedition onboard, consisting of 17 men, under the command of a naval captain, Herman Ritter. Five days later they reached Hansa Bay on Sabine Island, after an unsuccessful attempt to approach the coast further north. Hansa Bay proved a good hideout, screened by Pendulum Island on the seaward side, and protected by reefs. The ship was soon firmly in the grip of the ice, and transmission was carried out both onboard and ashore, where two huts were erected. An American plane from the "Northland" flew over the same day, but failed to spot them.

The trawler "Sachsen" had been sent to the south-east coast of Greenland to establish a meteorological station in June 1940, but in order not to provoke the USA unduly, it had been decided to make it a floating station, and transmission was carried out in the Denmark Strait in September of that year. Before a week had elapsed it was discovered that the Allies were trying to locate them by radar, and for this reason transmission was discontinued.

In the spring of 1941 the "Sachsen" was sent off to the same place, but this time its primary task was to investigate ice conditions, and in addition to report on any minefields and enemy air activity in the Denmark Strait in preparation for the anticipated break-out into the Atlantic of the battleship "Bismarck", whose fate meanwhile was sealed already on 27th May, 1941, when she was sunk by units of the Royal Navy, ably assisted by the RAF. After completing her mission in the Denmark Strait the "Sachsen" proceeded to the waters around Jan Mayen, and for three months continued to send weather reports enduring all the local discomforts of violent gales and icing conditions. In the Denmark Strait between Iceland and Greenland the ice conditions are better in winter than in summer, contrary to what one would expect.

Herman Ritter was born in Czecho-Slovakia, then part of the Austro-Hungarian Empire, and in 1938 annexed by Nazi Germany. He visited Svalbard in 1930 as a member of the Prince of Monaco's expedition, and subsequently made a living there as a trapper. He soon became familiar with the spirit of comradeship that existed among trappers, irrespective of nationality, and for this reason he was uneasy at the thought of having to make war on other members of the fraternity. He instructed his men to avoid killing anyone.

Ritter was not a Nazi, unlike Gottfried Weiss, who had joined the expedition as its scientist, and other members. Relations between them were therefore strained: Ritter experienced a sense of insecurity, having been formerly screened by the Gestapo, and was anxious for the safety of his family. Dr Rudolf Sensse, the expedition's medical officer, was more neutral.

When the Germans in Hansa Bay realised that their whereabouts had been discovered, they made haste to set off in pursuit. It was vital that no report should reach the radio station at Eskimones, in which case they could expect to be visited by Allied bombers.

Ritter, who was ill, went only as far as Germaniahavn, but Weiss was only too eager to continue the chase. When Jensen and his men were about to bunk down in the hut at Cape Wynn, the arrival of the enemy was somewhat belatedly announced by the exhausted sledge dogs. As the Germans were already on their way up from the ice there was no time to harness the dogs. Dashing out at the back of the hut, they ran up the hill in the dark, floundering in deep snow without their boots or outer garments, carrying only their rifles, which were of little use in the dark.

Marius Jensen ordered the two Eskimos to try to make their way back to Eskimones and report what had happened while he himself stayed on for a while to keep an eye on things, in the hope that the Germans would abandon their post. However, they stayed on in their hut. As an old trapper Jensen knew the importance of always carrying his rifle, and this stood him in good stead. As he made his way through deep snow over the brow of a hill and down the southern slope, he reached the shore, where the ice had been screwed into strange shapes. Making his way along he suddenly found himself face to face with a large polar bear. Both stopped in surprise and glowered at one another. Jensen was reluctant to shoot the animal, as this would reveal his presence to the enemy. He knew, too, that if he turned on his heels and made off, his number would be up; the beast would regard him as fair game, set off in pursuit and kill him with a blow of his giant paw. He stood stock still, staring at the bear, in the hope that it might shamble off, as often happens, but it remained rooted to the spot staring fixedly at Jensen. The latter advanced a few steps, but the bear was immovable. There was only one solution: with a well-aimed shot through the head Jensen felled his adversary. The sound of the shot echoed around the hills, and for a while he stood there listening, but an eerie silence prevailed. He now set out on the 150 kilometres return journey to Eskimones, where he arrived on 13th March suffering severe frost-bite, after incredible hardships negotiating the hummocked ice. Poulsen had spotted him as a tiny dot away out on the ice, without a dog-team, and realised that something was amiss. He despatched an Eskimo with a dog-team to bring him in.

The other two Eskimos had not yet returned. Defensive measures were now set on foot in case the enemy should make an appearance.

After Jensen and the two Eskimos had made their getaway, Weiss bided his time. He was convinced that they would have to return to fetch their equipment, which was vital if they were to survive. But he was wrong; all three managed to make their way back to Eskimones.

Weiss and his men were now left behind in the hut, and suddenly found themselves saddled with three dog teams. But no one had learnt how to handle them. The dogs were unaccustomed to German words of command and pulled in different directions. After a considerable time and much patience they were under sufficient control to enable the Germans to make their way back to the Hansa Bay base.

For patrolling the coast sledge dogs were important not only as draught-beast but also for their ability to scent living creatures, human or animal, at a considerable distance.

Spotting an enemy is easier, and when out hunting there's no difficulty in tracking game—muskox, bear and fox, though this could be risky. Once they scent a polar bear the dogs dash off at full speed, out of control. The bear, with his native cunning, will set off across the ice towards the open sea. All of a sudden the ice gives way and sledge and dog team sink to the bottom, and the driver will be lucky to get away with his life. This is particularly dangerous in the dark, when it is impossible to see what animal the dogs are chasing. A polar bear, when hunted, can outrun a heavy dog-sledge with ease, and for this reason the usual procedure is to let go a couple of dogs. These will catch up with the bear, and hurl themselves at their target, even though a blow from the bear's mighty paw could kill them. The dogs must not be released too soon, otherwise there will be no time to shoot the bear before it has slain them; but if the dogs are let loose too late and the bear is attacked, the beast will go for the dog team, which will be quite defenceless, being tethered to the sledge. In such cases quick action and a well-aimed shot are the only guarantee of survival.

The Germans concluded that, even if their whereabouts were known, the Eskimones radio station would have to be destroyed. It was essential that any bombers based in Iceland 1000 km distant should not receive the necessary weather reports on their way. After a week's training in dog-driving the detachment set off under the command of Ritter. In the evening of 23rd March they reached Eskimones just after nightfall, but were spotted when they were out on the ice.

While Poulsen, Olsen and Rudi were back in the hut with a number of Eskimos, the others were out on patrol. They were beginning to feel safe, as there had been no sign of the enemy, but had nevertheless made preparations for a possible attack. They now dashed out and took up their allotted defensive positions round the hut.

Ritter, who had picked up a certain amount of Norwegian during his time in Svalbard, had learnt a good deal from the logbook Marius Jensen had been forced to leave behind in the hut at Cape Wynn. As he moved towards the hut in the dark he was challenged by Poulsen and asked to identify himself. Instead of answering he asked if he could talk to Poulsen. When told that this was not possible, he asked to speak to Olsen or Rudi, whom he knew from his stay in Svalbard, but received the same answer. "Did they intend to defend themselves?" he asked. When Poulsen answers "Yes", they were met with a burst of machinegun-fire, with tracer bullets streaking in every direction. Poulsen fires at the presumed attacker, but this only served to attract another volley, and he dives for cover. No one has been hit, but there is no time to harness the dog-team. Making good their escape Poulsen and his men retire up the slope behind the hut, through deep snow, without boots and warm clothing. Left on his own, as the others had vanished, Poulsen now sets off on the 300–kilometre trek along the inner fjords to Ella Island, where there are people and a radio station, putting up at night en route in trappers' huts, woefully short of food and fighting desperately to stave off frostbite in his feet. After eleven days of extreme hardship and toil he literally slumped to the floor of the hut on Ella Island. The others from Eskimones had not yet arrived.

Ritter destroyed the radio station, and somewhat reluctantly set fire to the hut, anxious not to be reprimanded for leaving it in a serviceable condition. But one small hut was left standing, with enough provisions and equipment to enable anyone to survive in an emergency. When Ritter had been firing at the enemy he had been aiming around trying to scare them to surrender.

Ritter and his five companions now set off on their way back to Hansa Bay. They now had as many as 50 sledge dogs at their disposal. Another logbook he had found revealed that there were several Danes patrolling in the area, and for this reason he was constantly vigilant. When they reached the hut at Sandsodden, and were enjoying a rest, they suddenly caught sight of a man driving a dog-team. They waited till he was close at hand, and then approached and told him to stop. Taken by surprise the man shouted an order to his dogs, cracked his whip, and veered off. As he grasped his rifle he was hit by a bullet, and fell off his sledge, while the team raced on, dragging dead and dying dogs with them.

The man was Eli Knudsen: he had been hit in the chest, and died shortly after he had been carried into the hut.

Ritter was furious, and cursed the man who had fired the shot; he had ordered only to shoot the dogs; the latter insisted that his magazine had jammed, and the round had gone off of its own accord. Long after the event Ritter was quite disconsolate at what had occurred, blaming himself for the accident.

From the log-book he also knew that two other men were out on patrol and would probably be turning up. He and his men tidied up, and remained in hiding. His surmise proved correct: not much later Marius Jensen and his team of huskies arrived. Previous experience had made Jensen extra cautious about approaching a hut, but the sight of smoke curling up from the chimney persuaded him that Eli Knudsen had already arrived. He stopped, walked over to the hut without the slightest misgivings, and was taken completely unawares by the Germans. Shortly afterwards Petter Nielsen walked into the same trap.

Both men were now interrogated by Ritter, and gave a convincing account of themselves, without giving away anything of importance. They were taken back to Germaniahavn on the south side of Sabine Island by their captors, where they were kept closely guarded while all the time planning to escape.

Much to his surprise Ritter was sharply criticised by Weiss for burning down the hut at Eskimones, as this would give the Germans a bad reputation. This was an added source of worry: he was already afraid of Gestapo reprisals not only against himself but also his wife and children back in Germany. However, he allowed Petter Nielsen to make his way south to Sandodden to bury Eli Knudsen, and took Marius Jensen with him on a long trek north in the direction of Hochstetter Foreland as a relief from his more pressing problems and also with a view to finding a new site for the station. Something like friendship developed between these two men, based on their mutual love of life in the Arctic wilderness. Although he had plenty of opportunity to make good his escape, out of respect for Ritter Marius bided his time until he had a chance of leaving him in a safe spot. At the end of their long trek they reached Myggbukta, where they met Weiss, Dr Sensse and a few other men from the base. Weiss had planned to set off on his own initiative to Ella Island and destroy the radio station. Petter Nielsen, of course, was not at Sandsodden when they came past. Ritter's spirits were hardly improved after further rebukes from Weiss. When the latter set off, Marius Jensen gave him a certain amount of misleading information on the route south, which meant that he would take a good deal longer on the journey. But he himself needed to get there first, in order to warn them of Weiss's impending arrival. Shortly afterwards he managed to get hold of Ritter's rifle, and left him behind, with plenty of provisions but no sledge dogs or other means of transport, and then set off, as fast as he could go on the 140-kilometre trek to Ella Island, only to find that the place had been abandoned. Speeding back to Myggbukta, he fetched Ritter and once again sped south. Would they reach Ella Island before Weiss turned up? As luck would have it Weiss arrived a good deal later, and proceeded to destroy the station, though allowing the hut to remain standing, while Jensen made his way to Scoresby Sound with his captive Ritter, who felt a great sense of relief at being taken prisoner. His problems were solved, and as far as he was concerned the war was over.

Weiss now assumed command of the station in Hansa Bay. On 25th May it was bombed by American four-engined Liberators and Flying Fortresses from the Keflavik base in Iceland, in a raid led by the Norwegian-American aviator Colonel Bernt Balchen. After releasing their bombs the planes machine-gunned the station, setting fire to the radio building and a near-by hut, as well as the "Sachsen," which was frozen fast in the ice. The Germans, who had doubled to their defence posts, replied with bursts of anti-aircraft fire, but apparently to no effect. None of the Germans were hit. Later on they moved to a reserve camp at the foot of a steep hill, to ensure better protection against attack. A new wireless transmitter was set up and contact re-established; a Condor plane from Værnes, north of Trondheim, flew up and dropped supplies.

Now that summer had come, their station had been discovered, and fresh air attacks could be expected, there was no point in staying on. As it proved impossible to free their ship from the grip of the ice, Weiss radioed Norway and asked to be evacuated by air. When the ice broke up a six-engined Dornier 26 flying-boat landed in an open channel on 17th June. Before leaving the remaining huts were set on fire, and the "Sachsen" suffered the same fate, after the sea-cocks had been opened. As she burned, the ice around melted, and she went straight to the bottom.

Dr Sensse, however, had been left behind: he had made his way south to look for Ritter, of whose capture no one at the time was aware, and when he returned to Hansa Bay empty-handed the others had all left, leaving the place in ruins. Weiss had fortunately left provisions for him and Ritter.

At the end of July 1943 the ice-breaker "Northland," under the command of Ib Poulson, managed to reach Sabine Island, bringing men of the Sledging Patrol, who were landed. They came across a great deal of abandoned equipment and gutted huts in Hansa Bay. The frozen carcases of huskies were scattered around, still in their harness and with bullet holes in the head, while parachutes with red containers provided a splash of colour against the snow.

On the south side of the island near Germaniahavn they ran into a living human being sitting on a stone in company with an equally live huskie. He was lean, haggared and bearded and clearly at the end of his tether, clad almost entirely in rags and an anorak which bore the mark of a bullet shot at the shoulder. This was none other than Dr Sensse. On his trek to the south to look for Ritter he had gone through the ice, with his sledge and dog-team. His huskies were drowned but he had managed to reach dry land. The sledge had gone down with his warm outer clothing, which he had taken off owing to the warm weather that particular day. Fortunately he was not far from the Sandsodden hut, where he found the clothes that had belonged to Eli Knudsen, who had been shot there, as well as a few provisions. He had to stay there until the ice broke up; he was lucky enough to come across an old boat, in which he set out to row to Hansa Bay, a distance of about 45 miles.

The Sledging Patrol and the ice-breaker now set about searching for any other Germans who might have been left behind: it was not quite certain how they had managed to get away. There was dense drift-ice as far as the eye could see, and no ship would be able to enter, nor was there any suitable landing site for aircraft. A written message was discovered in which Weiss explained where provisions and equipment had been hidden.

There were certain indications that not all the Germans had left, and a search was set on foot. The "Northland" meanwhile was prevented by ice from sailing north. While they lay at anchor at Walrus Island just south of Sabine Island a huge iceberg came drifting down with the wind straight for the ship. Drift-ice made it impossible for them to move out of its path, and their ship was pressed up against a pebbly beach, with its keel scraping along the bottom. They were in a precarious position, and expected their ship to be crushed at any moment, when suddenly the colossus moved away, and with the aid of the anchor capstan and a powerful propeller they managed to work their way clear of the shore and reach a narrow open channel, after much bumping against ice and the sea floor. To the north Hochstetter Bay was covered with thick ice. Five men were put ashore at Lille Pendulum, an island to the east of Sabine Island, to keep an eye on things, and report back as soon as the ice broke up. The two huts on the Bass Rock just off shore were also investigated. Einar Mikkelsen and his friend were stranded here for 2 years, 1910–12, before they were rescued after the "Alabama" was crushed in the ice. A blizzard now sprang up, blowing from the north, driving the ice towards the shore, and threatening once again to force the "Northland" up against the land. To avoid this they set off at full speed to the south, trying to round Cape Borlase Warren to the bay south-east of Wollaston Foreland but just short of their goal they discovered a huge iceberg blocking their path. As they tried to nose their way in between two ice floes they struck a reef and went firmly aground. A mass of drift ice now threatened to crush the ship, but the situation was saved by dynamiting the ice ahead and clearing a passage which enabled the ship to take shelter in the bay.

As they were bringing provisions for the Sledging Patrol's hut at Zachenberg, they sailed on into Young Sound to the north of Clavering's Island. But here they were in shallow water, and a terrific jolt which shook the vessel and threw everyone off balance meant that they had struck a reef, and were now stuck fast. However, the rising tide floated them clear, and they continued on their way to the hut. A patrol with a dog team was landed, with orders to carry out a reconnaissance to the north, making its way over the Kuppel Pass all the way to Cape Berlin in the extreme north of Wollaston Foreland, which commanded views a long way to the north. But there was no sign of any Germans. Provisions were also deposited at Revet on the landward side of Clavering Island. Continuing round they reached Eskimones at Dead Man's Point on the south side, where a new station was projected to replace the one burnt down by Ritter, using material which the ice-breaker "North Star" was bringing up from Iceland, but was now reported to be trapped in the ice further south.

Meanwhile a helicopter was sent to Lille Pendulum to report on the detachment stationed there, and to drop supplies. They had built a stone hut on top of a hill some two or three hundred metres high, from which they commanded extensive views. As yet there was no sign that the ice was about to disappear. This is always difficult to predict and may suddenly occur. Three days later it happened; the ice broke up, and was drifting south. The "Northland" now got moving, thrusting her way north against the drifting ice bearing down on her. It took several days to reach Lille Pendulum, where the patrol was embarked. Continuing north they reached Cape Rink north of Hochstetter Bay on the landward side of Shannon Island, where there were uninterrupted views all around, and where a guard hut was erected later on.

In the winter of 1869–70, a German expedition had visited these parts under the command of Captain Karl Koldewey. One of his men, Lieutenant Payer, had discovered a coal seam several kilometres long further inland in the Ardencaple Fjord, at a spot named Kolhus, which has been an important source of fuel for surrounding trappers' huts. The "Northland" made her way in and took on board coal for all the Sledging Patrol's huts. The Ardencaple Fjord thrusts its way into the heart of the mountain massif, with impressive precipitous cliffs on either side, like the Kjerulf Fjord, further south, off the Franz Josef Fjord, where the beetling cliffs soar over 6,000 feet above the water.

Koldewey made his winter quarters in Germania-havn on Sabine Island, and was the first European to spend the winter in East Greenland. The previous year he had made an unsuccessful attempt to reach the coast, and made his way instead to Svalbard, which he circumnavigated via the Hinlopen Strait. In 1869 his expedition had arrived on the "Germania" and the "Hansa," but the latter had been trapped in the ice on 5th September, driven south and was crushed by the ice 14 days later off the Franz Josef Fjord. The crew set up a hut on an ice floe, and continued to drift along the coast until May of the following year (1870), after which they took to the boats, which they had brought with them, rounded Cape Farewell, and eventually reaching terra firma on 13th June on the south west coast of Greenland.

Clavering Island is named after the English naval officer D. C. Clavering, who arrived here in 1823 in the brig "Gripper," after a voyage round the coast of North Norway and Svalbard. At Eskimones he came across an Eskimo tribe of 12 persons, and on the beach he found a burial place which has given name to Dead Man's Point just beyond. One of the members of the expedition was a scientist by the name of Edward Sabine, who carried out a number of experiments on terrestrial magnetism and the length of the second's pendulum.

The crew of the "Northland" set up a hut on the site of an old settlement near Cape Rink, which was intended for use as an outpost for the Sledging Patrol. Search parties were sent out, and one of them found a German army tunic which Dr. Sensse declared was his, as he had been in the area on a reconnaissance mission the year before, although some doubt was cast on the truth of this.

They continued on their way north halfway along the Hochstetter Foreland as far as Høysåta, a mountain top in Rosenneath Bay, from the summit of which could be seen a vast expanse of country to the north, with nothing but ice and icebergs of all shapes to meet the eye.

It was now the end of August, too late in the year to proceed further north. A fresh storm was bearing down on them from the north, and they were forced to lie in the lee of a grounded iceberg all night long until the gale had blown itself out.

A few days later the ship was lying at anchor in Fredens Bay on the south side of Shannon. A plane was sent up to carry out a reconnaissance of the island, but immediately after take-off it started to blow a gale, with snow showers, and fears were expressed for the pilot as the aircraft disappeared from sight. As it also vanished from the radar screen, it was thought to have crashed. The gale subsided as suddenly as it had sprung up, and shortly afterwards the plane was seen returning. The pilot had found a natural landing strip at the foot of Tellplatte, a ridge on the southern end of the island. Reconnaissance next day revealed several footprints and an emaciated husky, which prompted the belief that the Germans had been evacuated by air. While the "Northland" was lying in the bay a German bomber suddenly appeared overhead, and the crew doubled to their action stations, but the plane veered off to the north.

The "Northland" now made her way south through the drift-ice in Hochstetter Bay, but once again she was trapped among large ice floes, and bore down on Lille Pendulum with the risk of being crushed against the rocks. While attempts were being made to find a way out the ship received a terrific jolt: the propeller had fouled the edge of the ice and been badly bent, so badly that it was almost useless. The situation was critical, as the ship hardly answered to her helm. In the end they managed to back away from the dangerous rocks, and now made their way back to Cape Rink and open water, where they could repair the damaged propeller. Meanwhile the ice was beginning to form round the ship, and it looked as if they might have to spend the winter there. On 1st September, however, the much hoped-for foehn wind arrived and they broke away and started butting their way through the ice, with frequent recourse to dynamite. It took them a whole night to work their way through the Pendulum Strait, but once again a storm, with flurries of snow and poor visibility, blew up and they had to shelter behind a stranded iceberg to ride out the gale.

Meanwhile they received a report that the icebreaker "North Star," on her way from Iceland and approaching Eskimones, was in difficulties, having broken her rudder, and was battling through the storm, while the drift ice was driving her towards the land. She needed assistance, but it was impossible for the "Northland" to do anything. The sealer "Polarbjørn," which had also come from Iceland, had already reached Eskimones, but she had no wireless listening watch just then. In a desperate bid to solve the problem, two bold spirits from the "Northland" undertook the hazardous flight through the storm, and dropped a message on the deck of the sealer, urging her to go to the assistance of the stricken vessel. "Polarbjørn" immediately set off and managed to tow "North Star" in to Eskimones.

It was now "Northland's" turn to try to get there, but once again she stuck fast in the ice. Pressure on her hull increased, and ice held her fast, pressing up along her sides and spilling onto the deck. For a whole week the ship drifted helplessly around, gripped by the ice, and preparations were made to abandon the vessel, but all of a sudden the ice relaxed its hold. Even so a couple of days had to be spent dynamiting, before they finally broke loose.

The two other ships left Eskimones after setting up the station for the Sledging Patrol's main base. From open water they ventured out into the ice, and tried to nose their way between the icefloes, but in vain: the ice closed in, and they drifted aimlessly. By the time they were free it was mid-September 1943, and high time to sail south. The ships needed to be overhauled after the gruelling treatment they had endured in the ice. The Sledging Patrol settled down at Eskimones in order to continue their vigilant sorties throughout the dark winter. They expected to have a quiet time, but when daylight returned next spring they would experience a dramatic encounter with the enemy.

The east coast of Greenland in the area around Shannon Island is one of the most perilous and difficult to navigate, owing to constant storms and unpredictable ice conditions. The stretch of sea between North Greenland and Svalbard provides the most important outlet for polar ice moving in a constant stream south in a broad belt some way off the coast, whereas there is generally open water nearer land. However, an easterly wind may at any moment propel the drift ice towards land, where it will pile up against any island or protuberance along the coast. Shannon Island, which is 50 km long and up to 40 km wide, is a typical example, stretching some way out from the coast and presenting a major obstacle to the southward drift of the ice.

The vast, cold inland ice cools down the air, producing fog and frequent storms. In some years with a prevailing easterly wind the ice will pile up in a barrier of impenetrable pack-ice, which even the most powerful icebreaker cannot penetrate. Over the years many a ship has attempted this task and been screwed down and crushed in the ice, with the loss of many lives.

Long experience, which a number of Norwegian sealing skippers acquired while operating along the east coast of Greenland, is necessary in order to negotiate the ice in these waters. Nosing one's way through cracks in the ice and thrusting the ice floes aside with the hull will often prove more efficient than running headlong into the ice. Some icebreakers are designed in such a way that they can run their bows onto the ice, pump water into the forepart of the vessel, and break the ice by sheer weight.

Norwegian skippers have often taken advantage of an easterly wind by setting off from North Cape for the west coast of Svalbard and into the drift-ice. At the same time by hoisting sail they have enjoyed a calmer passage than if they had steered due west from Tromsø, pitching and tossing in heavy seas.

In some years ice conditions have been so difficult that it has proved impossible to reach the east coast of Greenland: in 1943 and again in 1944 conditions were particularly unfavourable, as the account will show.

For the winter of 1943/44 the Germans dispatched another expedition code-named "Bassgeiger" to the east coast of Greenland on board the trawler "Coburg," accompanied by a U-boat, under the leadership of the meteorologist Heinrich Schatz, with Lieut. Helmuth Zacher as military commander. Skipper Rodebrugger had a crew of 18.

They sailed from Narvik on 27th August, and reached the drift-ice four days later at 77° Lat. N., and attempted to penetrate the ice, only to be stuck fast between two large floes. Attempts to dynamite a passage proved a laborious business: they drifted south with the movement of the ice, and after a week caught sight of the Ile de France and Germanialand. Additional supplies of explosives were dropped by plane, but further attempts at dynamiting were no more successful. Then they discovered that the ice had torn a half-metre-long rent in the bows: water poured in and much of their equipment was spoilt. They were forced to man the pumps for a whole day before the hole was patched.

After a few days the ship entered the pack-ice and pressure increased: further attempts at dynamiting were useless. The masts were unstepped and lashed alongside the hull for extra protection, and they now moved south with the ice, like a floating meteorological station. After a month the ice finally broke up, and they reached open water. They followed the ice edge south until they were off Cape Sussi on the northeast corner of Shannon Island, where they anchored. Ashore they came across a hut left behind by Einar Mikkelsen's Alabama Expedition 1909–12. It had been set up at Mount Meyersten, but was by now of little use.

The ship froze fast eight kilometres from land and a camp was set up on the ice, consisting of tents and igloos a little closer in. In November a storm blew up lasting several days, breaking up the ice, and almost crushing the "Coburg," which was driven against an iceberg with its bows canted up at an angle of 30° and its stern wedged in the ice. The whole party was forced to move over to the camp on the ice, although the transmitter onboard was in constant use. During the storm much of the equipment had been lost and this was replaced by fresh drops from the air.

At the end of November work was started on excavating a large cave,

40 by 30 metres, in a huge snowdrift ashore, and the arduous task began of transporting all the equipment all the way from the ship to the land-based camp, back-breaking work across the rough and hummocky ice, in sub-zero temperatures, in the dark, and freezing wind. Sledges were smashed against the jagged ice and the men were forced to hump their loads. At the beginning of January the radio equipment was brought ashore and transmission commenced in the cave, to the very end of February, the men toiled at the task of carrying all the equipment ashore. Inside the cave the men slept in low pup tents only a metre high, thus ensuring that the heat provided by small primus stoves would not allow the temperature to drop below minus 15°C. They all suffered continuously from the cold, and only emerged in order to carry out measurements. When transmission deteriorated owing to ice forming on the apparatus, this had to be moved across to a hut erected outside, after which transmission improved noticeably.

At the end of February 1944 the ice broke up in a violent foehn storm, in which the temperature soared from minus 32 to plus eight degrees in next to no time. The men encamped on the ice were forced to evacuate, some to terra firma and others to the "Coburg," which broke away from the ice, and drifted a number of miles to the south.

After the Germans had started transmitting, they were located by the radio-direction finding station Admiral Smith had established on Jan Mayen to monitor German activity in East Greenland. It had been secretly installed near Nordlagunen to avoid detection by German planes.

In the course of February 1944, as daylight returned, two members of the Sledging Patrol were sent north on a tour of inspection of the coast. On Shannon Island they came across sledge tracks in the snow, and realising that the enemy were bound to be in the vicinity, they hurried back to the hut at Cape Rink, and sent a message to Marius Jensen at Eskimones. He contacted the US base at Narsarsuak on the south-west coast, with a request for troops to be sent up. He assumed that they could be air-landed on flat Shannon Island. But bad weather set in and Jensen, impatient at this delay, decided to attack with his small force, as soon as the weather turned foggy. On 22nd April six men crept cautiously towards the German camp at Cape Sussi, to a spot where they commanded a view of the enemy outpost. Visibility, however, was poor, and Jensen advanced still further. Suddenly he heard a noise immediately behind him, and swivelling round found himself eye to eye with a German, who was just as astonished as himself. The German was the first to react, firing a shot which missed. Jensen was more fortunate and the German military commander, Lieut. Zacher met his death. A veritable shoot-out ensued, and the Danish patrol was forced to withdraw in the face of German superiority in fire power and numbers, while keeping the Germans under constant observation. The Danes were now stationed at the Cape Rink outpost, where a hut had been erected the previous autumn.

Captain Rodebrugger had assumed command after Zacher. The "Coburg" was abandoned in the ice on 6th May, and the remainder of the party put ashore. They were now ordered to prepare for evacuation, and on 3rd June a Junker 290 landed on a stretch of nice smooth ice south of the Alabama Hut in Nordenskiöld Bay, and transported them back to Trondheim.

In order to put an end, once and for all, to the great volume of German activity in East Greenland, the Americans despatched two large and modern ice-breakers —the "Eastwind" and the "Southwind," each of 6000 tonnes—as well as the Coast Guard vessels "Northland" and "Storis," in the summer of 1944. Owing to bad weather and difficult ice conditions they arrived too late to capture the "Bassgeiger" expedition.

When the "Northland," under the command of Lieut. R. F. Blutcher, approached Shannon Island in August 1944, it was found to be surrounded by solid ice on every side. Attempts to force a passage met with tough resistance. On the south side a little progress was made. In order to save time the commander of the US detachment, Captain Bruce Minnick, despatched a sledging patrol. When they reached the island, and started to climb the slope, they were caught in a sudden storm of rain and sleet, sinking into the wet snow with every step they took. Progress was so slow and arduous that they were forced to turn back. But on the level ground at the top of the slope they had found wheel-tracks in the snow, which might have been made by a large plane. Had the enemy been evacuated? Or had a plane brought supplies?

The "Northland" managed to force her way west to within a few nautical miles off Cape Sussi, and started to work her way towards the shore, where they discovered the "Coburg" locked in the grip of great blocks of ice. They reached a snow-covered stretch of ice running all the way to the shore but full of dangerous cracks. A section set off on foot, dragging a dinghy, and roped together, a necessary precaution as one of them fell through the ice and was quickly pulled out, while the dinghy enabled them to negotiate channels. On reaching the shore they saw the hut abandoned by the Germans, and approached cautiously, their side arms at the ready. Kicking in the door, they stormed in, only to find the hut empty. Only one German had been left behind: a German steel helmet on a wooden cross marked the grave of Lieut. Helmuth Zacher.

The "Northland" had damaged her propeller in the ice, and had to be escorted by the "Storis." The latter had assisted in moving the base of the Sledging Patrol to Sandodden, where a new hut had been erected and both a jeep and a motorboat had been deposited. This was the spot where Ritter had had his dramatic encounter with the Sledging Patrol the previous year.

A few days later the "Northland" arrived from the north, and abreast of Shannon Island the crew were surprised to see a trawler butting its way along the edge of the ice, and assumed that it was a German ship.

For the coming winter 1944/45 the enemy had planned a new expedition to East Greenland to relieve "Bassgeiger", and was code-named "Edelweiss" after its leader Gottfried Weiss, consisting of 11 men, most of whom had formed part of operation "Holtzauge" the previous year.

They sailed onboard the trawler "Kehdingen" all the way from Wismar, commanded by Edmund Polski and with a crew of 15. Leaving Tromsø on 27th August, 1944 they reached the drift ice on 31st August. On the following day, 1st September, they were surprised by the "Northland." The U-boat that had escorted the ship submerged before being discovered, while the "Kehdingen" made off at full speed into the drift ice pursued by the "Northland." To start with the German vessel drew away from its pursuer. Suddenly a tremendous explosion was heard astern of the "Northland" and a column of ice and water reared up. On recovering from the shock they concluded that it must have been a U-boat, and shortly afterwards it was spotted in a channel. Its torpedo had struck an ice-floe nearby. Captain Butcher resisted the temptation to set off in pursuit of the U-boat, as he considered the "Kehdingen" more important. He continued the chase, opening fire, and for several hours the hue and cry continued among the ice-floes, and gradually the "Northland" closed the distance. Finally the "Kehdingen" stuck fast in the ice 200 yards off Cape Alf Trolle, the southern extremity of Store Koldewey. After making desperate attempts to come clear, they realised that their number was up. After jettisoning secret equipment and documents, they scuttled their ship and tried to make their escape further into the drift ice on board two lifeboats, only to suffer the ignominy of engine failure. Defeat stared them in the face, and all 26 members of the expedition, after throwing their weapons into the sea, walked across the ice and surrendered, no doubt relieved that for them the war had come to an honourable conclusion, a war they realised would inevitably soon be lost.

Now that the Germans were fighting a losing battle it was particularly important for them to obtain weather reports from East Greenland. It was therefore to be expected that they would despatch a new expedition, this time probably further north and to a still more inaccessible spot. The American vessels consequently sailed north and made a rendezvous with the new ice-breaker "Eastwind" abreast of the southern extremity of Store Koldewey at Cape Alf Trolle, 76° Lat. N. The ice-breaker led the way, forcing a passage in through the ice belt with its powerful bows, until open water was reached on 13th September, 1944. The ships were commanded by Captain Charles Thomas on board the "Eastwind,' which carried three small aircraft that made reconnaissance flights along the coast. They reported that it was possible for the Germans to penetrate the ice all the way up to the Ile de France, and Captain Thomas despatched the two other ships to patrol the coast to the south. Wireless silence was ordered. He himself made his way first of all into Dove Bay with all its inshore islands, and then up to Mörkefjorden, where the sledging patrol maintained an outpost consisting of two men. This fjord cuts deep into the mainland. He now decided to take part in a reconnaissance flight to Germania Land in the north as far as Skjaerfjorden, but unfortunately the plane developed icing problems over a glacier and rapidly lost height. After narrowly avoiding crashing on the shore it managed to come down on the thin ice covering the fjord. Further north he found ice conditions better than expected, with no sign of the dreaded pack ice. He managed to penetrate as far north as 80°, and claimed to have sailed in "Eastwind" further north up the east coast of Greenland than anyone had previously done, after passing the Belgica Bank, a spot named after the ship of the Duke of Orleans which was here in 1902.

When an ice-breaker was ordered to relieve him he turned south again. "Southwind," the new sister-ship, was on her way from Boston to replace "Northland" and "Storis," which needed to proceed to Iceland for repairs. Off Shannon "Eastwind" ran into a full gale, with heavy seas and snow showers. She ran for the lee of Cape Philip Broke on the southern tip of the island, after one of the planes had broken loose and been smashed. Worse was to follow: a message was received that the "Northland" had broken her steering cable and was drifting out of control off Hochstetter Bay. Braving the elements "Eastwind" fought her way through the darkness to reach the stricken vessel, succeeded in getting a towline on board, and with great difficulty towed "Northland" through heavy seas to the comparative calm of the Pendulum Strait and ice-free water, where the necessary repairs could be carried out once the storm abated.

As "Southwind" was on her way Captain Thomas considered that he no longer needed the smaller ships, and that they should proceed south to Iceland before risking getting stuck in the ice and being forced to break wireless silence. On 30th September "Eastwind" commenced clearing a channel through the ice-belt, followed by "Evergreen", which had "Northland" in tow, and "Storis" astern as a protection against U-boats. After 18 hours they were through. The ice-breaker returned and found open water off Shannon, and aerial reconnaissance was resumed to the north. On 2nd October the pilot reported that he had observed a ship 100 nautical miles north, and that he had been fired at as he flew over it. It was situated to the north of Lille Koldewey in the strait between Store Koldewey and Germanialand. The ship in question was obviously German; the question was whether it had already disembarked an expedition, and was on its way back, in which case an attempt must first be made to seize the vessel. The expedition could then be dealt with afterwards. Once again the pilot, McCormick, flew north with an observer. His progress would be monitored on radar, and when the ship was spotted the plane had instructions to circle overhead. Meanwhile radio silence was maintained on board. But on this occasion there was no sign of the ship. Store Koldewey was shrouded in fog. "Eastwind" now sailed north, butting her way through the drift ice, which became increasingly difficult to negotiate throughout the night. Dawn revealed a mass of ice floes and icebergs as far as the eye could see. After a channel had been cleared in the ice the plane set off once again, and this time returned with good news: a pile of equipment and building material had been observed at Lille Koldewey, but no sign of the enemy. As soon as it was dark "Eastwind" set off, butting her way through the ice, for Lille Koldewey. Early next morning a detachment was landed on the firm ice bordering the northernmost of the two islands comprising Lille Koldewey. Moving cautiously across uneven country they surprised the Germans, who surrendered immediately. Their leader, Lieutenant Schmied, tried to set fire to a bag, on which he had poured petrol, but thanks to prompt reaction on the part of the Americans it was retrieved undamaged, and found to contain a mass of valuable secret papers, including the operational plan for arctic waters, U-boat codes, a land mine map for German stations, as well as meteorological and scientific observations. And finally, not least important, information on German naval forces in the Arctic.

The expedition had originally been intended for Novaya Zemlja, and had been code-named "Goldschmied", but with the capture of "Edelweiss" it had been switched to East Greenland, and renamed "Edelweiss II". Its leader was Karl Schmied. It left Tromsø on 26th September, 1944, in thick fog onboard the 800-ton trawler "Externstein," under the command of Lieutenant Gerhard Rother, and with a crew of 18, while the actual expedition numbered 12 members. An escorting U-boat turned back once the ice had been reached on 30th September. The very next day the "Externstein" was trapped in the drift ice as she tried to force her way through; however, a warm wind from the west opened up a gap in the ice, and the ship made her way as far in as Lille Koldewey. Spurred on by the threat of enemy aircraft they hurriedly landed all their equipment, using lifeboats lashed together, which were towed ashore. Working at night as well, they had everything safely on land, in time for the ship to cast off in the afternoon of the next day. Almost immediately the sound of an aircraft engine was heard, and the plane from the "Eastwind" appeared overhead. After firing some shots the "Externstein" set off and was soon into the ice.

On 4th October, as already recounted, the "Eastwind" arrived and made the Germans prisoners. The "Externstein," however, had made her getaway.

McCormick was sent off on several reconnaissance flights to look for the elusive ship, but without success. On one occasion, returning to the "Eastwind," he was on the point of drowning, falling into the water as his plane was hoisted onboard. He drifted under an ice floe, but was sucked out by the propeller.

It required three days to get all the German equipment on board— large quantities of arms, wireless and meteorological gear as well as provisions for at least two years. This was all turned over to the Greenland authorities.

Captain Thomas was anxious to continue the search for the German ship. On 9th October he met the sister-ship "Southwind" in Hochstetter Bay, and they joined forces in the attempt to locate their prey. Meanwhile the captured Germans and the secret documents were sent off to Iceland onboard the "Storis".

Dr Karl Schmied was a keen mountain-climber and an expert on arctic conditions. He had taken a doctorate, and taught geography at the University of Stuttgart. He had looked forward to an opportunity to spend a winter in Greenland, and to transmit much needed weather reports to his native Germany, which was now fighting desperately to stave off defeat. He thanked Captain Thomas for the humane treatment he and his men were receiving, but refused to divulge any information beyond what was contained in the captured documents.

In common with many others Karl Schmied had attended the training centre at Goldhobe in the Riesengebirge which Knoespel had set up for personnel earmarked for arctic expeditions.

In the German documents Captain Thomas discovered a reference to another expedition, "Haudegen". Maybe this was to be sent off to Greenland after the demise of "Edelweiss II"? He would have to keep his eyes open.

Meanwhile he hoped that a storm would blow up and clear a passage through the pack-ice, and, hey presto, the storm duly arrived. Once it was over "Eastwind" found herself in the Pendulum Strait, which was free of ice. McCormick and an observer were sent off, and $1\frac{1}{2}$ nautical miles off Cape Borgen, the northern tip of Shannon, the ship was finally run to earth. She was lying well camouflaged among hummocks and screw ice, and was at first difficult to spot, not least because of the shadows cast by nearby icebergs and the black and white strips painted on her hull.

The "Eastwind' set off at once. There was no time to lose: winter was drawing on, and fresh ice was beginning to form. In a couple of weeks' time the operation would be impossible. Both ships forced their way through the clogging ice, searching constantly for open channels, but for most of the time buffeting their way against the ice, reversing and renewing the assault, as the ice grew thicker and thicker. When darkness fell it was difficult to see what obstacles lay ahead, and ship and crew suffered a severe shaking. Gradually they neared their target, which could just be seen on the radar screen among the icebergs and hummocks, which were also visible. At a range of 4000 metres they opened fire, at the same time shooting up starshells which provided a superb panorama of the arctic scene. After a couple of extra salvos, a flare sent up by the enemy indicated that they were surrendering. But the problem now was to reach the ship, which was firmly stuck in the ice. The simplest solution would be to scuttle her, but on balance this was rejected. Most of the night was spent getting closer to the ship, and Captain Thomas now ordered Captain Montrello of the Marines to make his way across the ice with a detachment and take the crew prisoners, while he would continue to butt his way through the ice.

The crew of the "Externstein" were taken onboard the "Eastwind," but Captain Gerhard Rother remained in his ship, and Captain Thomas went onboard to meet him, and find out what had happened. The German proved to be a giant of a man, a pleasant character who was quite willing to talk. He had previously commanded oil tankers, and spoke English fluently. After they had been spotted by the aircraft on 2nd October, they had immediately made their way east through the ice, at the same time applying camouflage paint to the hull. The ice proved more and more impenetrable, and after a few days they were stuck fast. They prepared to scuttle their ship, and make their escape on skis and with an ice boat. They never thought the enemy would ever be able to reach them, and were greatly surprised when the first few shots rained down on them. "We could have shot down the plane when it was overhead, but refrained from doing so, as we felt quite safe." He soon had to change his mind. He had burned various papers in the ship's furnace, and bombs had been placed in readiness to sink the ship. When it was light, the prospects of getting the German ship clear of the ice appeared hopeless, and even the icebreaker's chances seemed doubtful. Once again the Captain and his crew discussed the possibility of scuttling the enemy vessel, but the majority were against it, as they were keen to bring it with them as a prize of war, and it was agreed to make the attempt.

A fresh captain and crew took possession of the "Externstein," which at the same time was re-christened the "Eastbreeze," in a traditional ceremony using genuine French champagne from the ample German stores onboard. The struggle to escape from the ice could now begin, "Eastwind" clearing a passage up to the stem of the other vessel and towing it astern with extreme caution, as one of her propellers had been damaged. Not before 17th October did they reach "Southwind," which had been lying in Hochstetter Bay awaiting their arrival after the damage she had sustained. On they went, in line astern, "Eastwind" leading the way and clearing a channel through the ice, assisted by the aircraft which would occasionally take off in a search for open water, as well as keeping an eye open for enemy ships. Three days later they eventually reached the open sea, where they ran into gale-force winds and heavy seas. "Eastbreeze," which was in need of repairs, was armed and sent to Iceland, arriving on 30th October, and docking six weeks later in Boston, Mass., USA's first prize in World War Two.

This expedition marked the end of the "weather-reporting war" in East Greenland. Germany's prospects were steadily declining, and no fresh expedition was dispatched to these shores. Meanwhile Captain Thomas and his ice-breakers searched in vain for Germans along the coast.

The Arado Caterpillar aeroplane AR232A with 10 pairs of wheels.

The polar bear on the beach. Capt. Ullring to the left, the author to the right.

German Meteorological Station at Signehavn at midnight.

The German ship "Coburg" stuck in the ice.

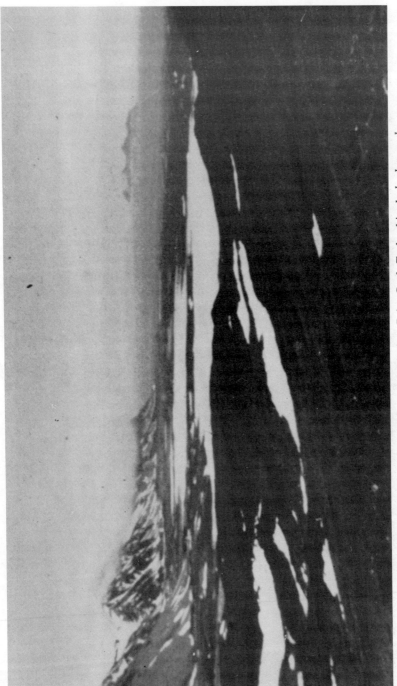

The Dieset-sletta seen from the summer station. Prins Carls Forland in the background.

Signehavn

Ltn. Healy and his crew.

Barentsburg, Spitsbergen.

The Advent Valley and Bay 1942. The Airstrip is somewhat unclear.

Longyearbyen, Spitsbergen.

Ny Aalesund—Kings Bay—with the hangar used for the airships "Norge" and "Italia".

Captain Ernst Ullring in Barentsburg upon leaving for U.K.

West Greenland

In 1942 Bernt Balchen, the Norwegian-born aviator who had acquired a great deal of experience of polar flying, not least on Admiral Byrd's south pole expedition of 1929, was promoted to the rank of colonel in the US Army Air Force, and entrusted with the task of establishing an air base and weather-reporting centre on the west coast of Greenland.

"Bluie West 8" base was set up in a fjord halfway along the coast, to be followed by B.W.1 near Julianehaab a fair distance to the south. These bases proved to be valuable intermediate landing stages, handling a large volume of traffic after the USA entered the war. After crossing the desolate inland ice-cap, planes would proceed to an intermediate landing in Iceland.

A great many aircraft came to grief in storm and fog, and Balchen's experience stood him in good stead in numerous rescue operations. A great many lives were saved, but many, too, were lost. Occasionally he was able to use the American-designed Catalina flying-boat, sometimes referred to as the Consolidated. This was capable of landing on the small lakes that sometimes formed on the top of a glacier when ice and snow melted in the sun, although this involved an element of risk, as a crevasse might suddenly open up in the ice, and the lake would disappear, leaving the flying boat standing on the dry ice.

In July 1942, 4 four-engined Flying Fortresses en route from Labrador were due to make an intermediate landing, but lost their bearings in dense fog. One plane landed safely, another crashed in the sea, but its crew were rescued, and a third made a forced landing without loss of life. Despite an intense search no trace could be found of the fourth plane, which was assumed to be lost. Next morning, however, it radioed to report that it had landed on the glacier, but had no idea just where. When the fog cleared Balchen took off, and spotted the plane some three miles from a small lake. Returning to base he fetched sledges and dogs and landed on the lake. Fog compelled him to spend the night in a tent on the edge of the water, but next day the rescue party made its way to the stranded aircraft, negotiating rugged terrain pitted with crevasses and strewn with blocks of ice, wading through streams of icy water. Intermittent fog reduced visibility, but Balchen's knack of finding his bearings in the polar wastes never deserted him. Deceptive bridges of snow across crevasses will often give way under the weight of a man, plunging him into the depths below, a fate that befell quite a number during the war in the Arctic. Not before nightfall did they reach their goal. Provisions and sleeping-bags had already been dropped to the crew of fourteen. The trek back to the lake proved an arduous one, even though the ground had frozen hard during the night. By the time they reached the rescue plane, which brought them safely to the base, they were utterly exhausted. A plane flying over the spot next day reported that the temporary lake had disappeared.

On 5th November, 1942, a transport plane with a crew of six disappeared on its flight over the inland ice-cap. A B 17 Flying Fortress which took off to search for the missing plane was itself reported missing. The first one was never found. After an intense search the B 17 was finally located on a glacier, over three thousand feet up, to the west of Angmassalik, just south of the Arctic Circle. It had come to rest above a huge crevasse, with its wings resting on the sides of the crevasse, and the tail section broken and suspended above the chasm. It was impossible to land anywhere near, as the ice was heavily crevassed all around. Provisions and equipment were dropped, a good deal of which was lost in the storm. In dense fog the plane had crashed on the ice, and several of the crew had been injured: one had broken both hands, while another had been hurled through the nose of the plane onto the ice, and been badly hurt. For several days storms forced them to remain inside the plane, but when two of them went outside to take stock of their situation, one of them suddenly disappeared down a crevasse, after stepping through the snow covering a treacherous "bridge" of ice. He landed on a shelf a hundred feet down. With the aid of a rope made of parachute lines he was hauled to safety.

An amphibian plane managed to land about a kilometre away, and two of those who were able to walk were rescued. Next day the plane returned and fetched two more, but in the fog it flew straight into a mountainside, and all three on board were killed.

Two wireless operators from a radio station down by the coast were then despatched with motor sledges. They arrived the very same day, but as they approached the plane, one of the motor-sledges suddenly crashed through the snow and disappeared down a crevasse. The sledge could be seen a long way down, but there was no sign of the wireless-operator. The navigator on board the marooned plane was suffering from frost-bite in both legs, as he had failed to remove snow that had collected in his boots when he and a few others had rescued the crew member who had been hurled out of the plane. He was in very considerable pain, and was placed on the remaining sledge so that he could be taken to a doctor as quickly as possible. Two of the crew went with them. After a few miles one of them suddenly disappeared down a crevasse, with no hope of being rescued, and a few miles further on the engine petered out, and as a gale blew up they were forced to pitch a tent. This was spotted by a plane, and provisions were dropped. Uninterrupted storms and dense fog now made further rescue attempts impossible, although several planes that ventured to try crashed.

Not until the beginning of February of the following year (1943) did Colonel Balchen succeed in making a belly-landing in a Catalina flying-boat on the ice not far from the tent, coming to a halt in the thick of a snowdrift. He managed to get three men on board his plane, but when he tried to take off, he discovered that his plane was frozen fast on the ice. Two of his crew had to get down onto the ice, and by rocking the aircraft—bearing down hard on alternate wings—they freed it, but when they tried to take off they found that they were once more stuck, so now they rocked the plane and revved up the engine at the same time. Slowly it gathered speed, and the two men outside had to run alongside and heave themselves onboard. The navigator, who had been lying in the tent for three months with frost-bitten legs, was in a lamentable condition, half his normal weight. He was flown back to the USA as soon as possible, where he had to have both legs amputated.

The three men now left in the B 17 were in constant fear that their plane, perilously perched astride a crevasse, would disintegrate and vanish. To prevent this they wound rope round the hull to hold it together, and were careful to be roped together. They were kept constantly supplied with provisions that were parachuted down.

Continued gales prevented further rescue operations until Balchen, in the middle of March, despite the atrocious weather, took off in a Catalina carrying dogs and sledges. Once again he made a belly-landing on the ice, and set off across the treacherous terrain with extreme caution. It took him 14 days of ceaseless fog and storm to bring the three men back to the rescue plane, but the Catalina refused to budge: it was frozen fast in the ice and too heavily ladened. In an attempt to take off one engine caught fire, but was repaired next day, when all unnecessary equipment was jettisoned. With only the second pilot and the three rescued men on board, the plane took off from the ice and flew back to base. Balchen himself was going to conduct the others down to the coast on foot. But once again they were storm-bound for over a week, sheltering in a tent at an altitude of over 3000 ft, before they finally completed the descent and flew back to Bluie West.

Operations on the west coast of Greenland and on the glaciers did not constitute an ordinary war, face to face with the enemy, but they were no less important to the outcome of the conflict: they helped to protect and ensure a constant flow of material, planes and men from west to east. Great courage, endurance and self-sacrifice in saving the lives of others were shown by men living in exceptional conditions. Loss of life could as a rule be ascribed to their ignorance of arctic conditions.

Greenland's geographical position, comprising a huge cold barrier to air currents forced upward and cooled down, accounts for its prevailing climate of fog and gales.

No direct contact with the enemy took place on the west coast of Greenland. On one occasion a Folke Wulf 200 had circled the base, and for a while Balchen feared that the Germans might launch an air attack after they had arrived on the east coast.

In Svalbard the period that ensued after the Signehavn episode was comparatively quiet, involving routine work, medical checks of service personnel and an occasional trip to Longyearbyen. On 8th July a Catalina arrived with a number of newcomers, returning to the UK with Ullring, Reksten and a few others.

Practically every day we saw or heard German weather planes; now that Signehavn had been destroyed they were more dependent on aerial observations than ever.

The Germans were probably anxious to place an automatic met. station in Billefjorden, an arm of Isfjorden, as a Ju 88 was observed from Longyearbyen flying up the fjord and apparently dropping containers. A few days before, a German U-boat on its way up the fjord had been fired on.

I went with a detachment in a motor-launch that proceeded as far as Pyramiden, the Russian mining town at the head of Billefjorden. There was no trace of life, and nothing unusual to be seen, just abandoned houses and installations in a short narrow valley between towering mountains.

At Barentsburg large-scale excavation was started in order to contain the fire in the heaps of coal; besides we needed coal for use during the coming winter. It was difficult and strenuous work. For electricity we relied on a diesel plant near Finneset.

On 24th June two British seamen were buried at Russekeila near Cape Linné. They were from the ship that had gone down off South Cape (Sydkapp) in November 1941, and had managed to reach Cape Linné before freezing or starving to death. Their bodies had frozen, and were well preserved.

114

Friction among officers living in camp is by no means uncommon; under special conditions, such as ours, in an exposed outpost, it was almost inevitable.

An army officer had been placed under the command of a naval officer, a situation which both of them must have considered somewhat unusual. Captain Trond Vigtel, in charge of the army contingent, felt that the governor Bredsdorff interfered unduly in his decisions, and accordingly protested. As a result he was deprived of his command at Barentsburg, "exiled" to Longyearbyen, and replaced by his second-in-command Lieutenant Arnljot Lid.

Later on, when Bredsdorff arrived in Longyearbyen on a tour of inspection, Vigtel was posted to Sveagruva, in order to avoid a confrontation. Meanwhile a second-lieutenant, who was bold enough to criticise the governor for his treatment of Vigtel, was promptly confined to barracks, in this case a drilling tower some way up the mountain, where he remained for a whole day, pondering his indiscretion. If nothing else, he had a superb opportunity of studying the geography of Svalbard.

The governor must have possessed a very special sense of humour. He was not particularly diplomatic in his conduct, had a tendency of asserting the superiority of the navy over the army, which was not exactly calculated to endear him to a community composed largely of army personnel.

Every evening he could be seen, in company with the dentist, making his way down to the quay for the time-honoured ritual of spitting in the sea. The dentist was no doubt an entertaining companion, but he wore also a uniform of the right colour.

The governor's popularity was hardly enhanced when he confiscated a consignment of drinks that Reksten had presented to the mess. This caused a good deal of resentment, but in view of the conditions under which we were living, this was probably a correct decision. We were later to be forcibly reminded how important it was to be vigilant. No one anyway wanted to experience a new Pearl Harbour.

We had plenty of opportunity to enjoy a bit of shooting. On the north side of Isfjorden, near Alkhornet, were large flocks of eiderduck, and in the hills above the camp plenty of ptarmigan in the autumn. Later on we were compelled to go for bigger game, reindeer and muskox—in order to provide fresh meat. The cliffs teemed with bird life, above all gulls and auks, and puffins, those delightful birds with their parrot-like beaks.

The German Attack,
8th September, 1943

At 0145 hours GMT the alarm is sounded. As I come out onto the steps I am told that at Cape Heer ships have been sighted in Isfjorden, and almost immediately afterwards I spot two ships on their way in.

More ships come into view, and Bredsdorff, Watson and I discuss their identity. We have had no advance warning.

They are flying no national flag; surely they are German?

Bredsdorff orders Lieut. Lid, who has joined us, to man the guns. The other troops are ordered to retire up the slope behind the coal heaps by the radio hut. A 40 mm anti-aircraft gun, Bofors II, is mounted at the end of the heap.

Two of our men are confined to bed in the sick-bay in the uppermost barracks: Sverre Amundsen has his left leg in plaster after a knee operation, while Mathisen has a lung infection, but is well on the way to recovery, and is ordered to get dressed and join the others. Sigurd Kristoffersen has broken his right ankle, but has a "walking" plaster, and is on duty at the telephone switchboard.

The dentist and the medical corporal carry Sverre Amundsen on a stretcher and place him behind the coal heap. Sick and wounded ought really to be conveyed up Sykehusdalen, but Bredsdorff decides that there is no time.

By now we can see nine ships: a battleship and two destroyers sail past Cape Heer and into Isfjorden, while three destroyers round Festningen in line astern, and steam towards Barentsburg. Further down Isfjorden another battleship and two destroyers heave-to in sight, and take up station at the entrance to Grønnfjorden.

There is no longer any doubt that these ships are German, but Watson is still clinging to the hope that they might turn out to be British.

I deposit a few personal belongings beneath a broken crane, where I keep a reserve store of medical supplies, and then fetch my rucksack and Medical Companion before taking cover behind the coal heap.

From the fjord comes the boom of cannon, but for the moment no projectile comes our way: the Germans have opened fire on the radio station at Cape Linné, in the mistaken belief that it is manned. After sending in a detachment to take prisoners, and finding no one there, they proceed to level the station to the ground with their guns.

The coal heap is a hundred metres long, running south-west from the hillside, and forming a sort of trench with the slope behind, while at the same time providing protection against the outer waters of the Grønnfjorden. Innermost on the coal heap stands the wireless hut, covering the entrance to the mine.

The men are spread out along the entire length of the trench. The medical corporal and Amundsen on his stretcher are by the hut, well protected from the sea. The governor takes up his position near the gun, ready to issue the fire order.

Second-Lieut. R. Breidablikk is manning the Bofors. We also have a machine-gun, and below the coal heap Second-Lieut. Holmbo-Eriksen is in charge of a 20 mm Oerlikon anti-aircraft gun. A Bofors III, which is too exposed, is not being manned. Down the slope, by the extreme north end of the settlement stands a four-inch cannon. Second-Lieut. N. Engeset has orders to fire away as soon as the Bofors II opens up. Cape Heer has orders to fire if fired on.

Two destroyers are heading straight for us, while the third makes for Finneset further in. The German naval ensign has been broken out, and the decks are crammed with soldiers.

There is a deathly hush. The leading destroyer is now so close to the shore that it is screened by the slope, and cannot be hit by the cannon—a smart manœuvre—while the other can still be covered by the four-inch gun. We wait expectantly. Any moment now the balloon will go up.

"Fire!" Bredsdorff raises his arm. The first salvo from the cannon on the slope is aimed too high, but the next one makes a clearly visible hole in the side of the destroyer, and at the same time projectiles from the other gun sweeps its decks, and the destroyer receives two more hits.

All the enemy ships reply with every piece of ordnance at their disposal, and at the same time back away. The din is deafening.

After the fourth round the four-inch gun jams, and for the moment the crew are forced to retire. The volume of fire from the sea is intense, but Engeset and his men refuse to give up, returning to fire off a few more shots that find their mark.

The Bofors gun is blazing away non-stop, getting in a total of 150 rounds, and to counter this threat the ships now concentrate their fire on the coal heap. Shells, many of them tracer, explode repeatedly on the slope behind us, and some of the gun crew retire, despite Breidablikk's protests.

The battleship, which turns out to be the "Tirpitz," has hove in to the fjord, and is firing her fifteen-inch guns, which explode with a bang not far away.

Two Arado float planes are launched from the battleship, which skirt the cliff behind us, firing their guns. The flash of flame erupting from the gun-muzzles is clearly visible. But we make a 180 degree turn with our Bofors cannon, fire a salvo, and the planes disappear.

Blood is dripping onto my hand. I get up and walk around quite unaffected by all the shooting. I am in a state of euphoria. A piece of shrapnel has passed through the left side of my steel helmet, ploughing a furrow across my scalp and splitting it.

Sergeant Thyvold helps me apply a field dressing. As I sit down I see Barentsburg enveloped in smoke and flame. Bofors III, which is unmanned, gets a direct hit, and disintegrates with a roar.

We have been firing away for half an hour, but visibility is poor, and the Governor gives the order to cease fire. The wireless hut is burning, but we quickly douse the flames.

The Germans land troops at Barentsburg and Finneset, intending to carry out a pincer movement, and we send troops forward to counter this, but fire from the destroyers is so intense that they have to pull back.

Thyvold, who has been performing valiantly on the Bofors II, is now told by the Governor to take a few men with him and move down to the Bofors III, where there is also a machine-gun, and see what he can do.

He has to make his way down alone, reaches the machine-gun and starts firing away at the troops that are coming ashore. A plane makes a bee-line for him; Thyvold fires, and registers a hit on the Arado, which dives away towards the sea, while Thyvold deals with another plane. The first one manages to land near Finneset, and shortly after takes off.

Some of our men try to take to higher ground, after retiring south along the school and a timber stack, while others seek cover in a derelict adit highway up the slope. They are taken prisoner by the troops landed at Finneset, where a few hundred Germans were put ashore.

Some of the men manage to reach the hills, where they are pursued by German troops and aircrafts who ground-strafe them.

Others make their way up on the north side of the settlement, up Sykehusdalen, including the crew of the four-inch gun. These are pursued by the fifty odd Germans put ashore at Barentsburg. In the hills some are captured, killed or wounded.

The rest of the men behind the coal heap are ordered to withdraw into the mine behind the wireless station, and Medical Corporal Kristiansen is instructed to carry Amundsen in on his stretcher. I am standing by the gun, but finally the Governor persuades me as well to take cover in the mine, leaving only himself and Watson outside.

They make their way to the office in the uppermost barracks, which is still undamaged. The rest of Barentsburg is burning, they have to destroy some important papers, but are captured by the Germans.

Those were clearly the papers the Germans had in mind when for the time being they spared the office building: they were obviously well informed.

The adit is so encrusted with ice that we have to worm our way in on our stomachs. Kristiansen has had some trouble getting the stretcher in. The reason for the formation of ice is due to the fact that the average temperature in Svalbard is minus 10 degrees Centigrade, and in summer warm and humid air condenses and freezes when it comes into contact with rock.

But the further in we get, the less ice there is, until finally we're in a part of the mine that is dry, a bit warmer and free from ice.

As a rule it is estimated that the temperature rises one degree for every 30 metres from the surface.

About 20 yards in I come across the others: the patient on his stretcher is in good shape, and I inquire if there are any wounded. No. We loll around for a bit, but it's rather damp, and one or two of the men reconnoitre further in, returning to announce the discovery of an ice-free mine gallery a few hundred yards further in, where it's possible to stand upright. In our present shelter we have to crouch.

We withdraw to the lateral gallery, where we shall be safe, should the Germans start firing into the mine entrance. The main gallery continues further in. Second Lieut. Pedersen, our wireless operator, and Sergeant Lund have been exploring, and have found gas there. From another narrow passage that runs inward and downward we note a draught of fresh air. I send Kristiansen and Sergeant Vasseng, both experienced mining people, off to look for a possible exit, and they return half an hour later to report that they got as far as a door they failed to open.

It's cold inside. After waiting for six–seven hours I take Second Lieut. Pedersen with me to the entrance. Have the Germans departed?

At 1015 hours GMT we see the last of the German ships sailing off down Isfjorden. The whole of Barentsburg is on fire, but the wireless station and all its apparatus are strangely enough unscathed. The adjoining hut, where ammunition for the Bofors II was stored, is burning, with shells exploding incessantly and throwing up a shower of sparks around the wireless hut, setting fire to a number of beams connecting the two buildings. As there at first seems little hope of saving the wireless hut, we dash inside and start carrying out the apparatus.

While I'm busy getting the wireless equipment out, Pedersen hurries back into the mine. Once the hut is blazing anyone inside the mine would be in real danger, as it opens right on to the hut.

By the time the others have come out the explosions have died down. Approaching from the front we manage to saw off the burning beams and save the hut.

Twenty-two of us had been inside the mine, all in good shape, though a bit numb with cold. The whole of Barentsburg is a burning, smoking ruin. Only chimney stacks and the skeleton of the administrative building are left standing.

We immediately sent out a patrol to look for dead and wounded. No wounded were found in Barentsburg, but four dead: K. A. Lundin, A. K. G. Bernsten, Anton Nilsen and David Rae (British).

At 1330 hours GMT Lieut. Lid and a few others came down from the hills, followed at intervals by several others in small parties. We were told that Sergeant K. Nore had been wounded, but was now being carried down, and that John Kvalbein had been killed. Men were immediately dispatched to fetch the body.

Nore had been hit by a machine-gun bullet fired from a plane. The projectile had drilled a hole in his helmet, struck his head behind his right ear, ploughed a deep furrow running along the soft tissue in the front of his ribcage, and come to rest in a small exit aperture. Later we discovered that he had lost the hearing of his right ear and that his sense of balance had been impaired, probably due to fracture of the temple bone involving damage to the eighth cerebral nerve on the right hand side.

Nore was very much the worse for wear, and was placed in the wireless hut with Amundsen, but he made a speedy recovery, though he was confined to bed, where he passed the time reading. As he had lost the use of his right hand, owing to damage of the nerve at the neck, he learnt to turn the pages with a stick held in his mouth.

Apart from the wireless hut the research station was repaired after a fashion and used to house some of the men. Ten men were placed in a hut still standing at Cape Heer, and fifteen in a hut at Cape Laila near Coles Bay further in Isfjorden. In this way we managed to find accommodation for all the survivors. A party was also sent out to look for survivors, and as it approached Cape Laila near Coles Bay a strange incident occurred: a few men ran out of the hut, and set off up the hill. A fresh expedition found the dentist and a couple of others in the hut. Unaccountably they hadn't realised that the Germans had departed. After all, they must have seen the ships from Adventfjorden sailing past.

Out of a total of 95 men all told at Barentsburg and Cape Heer five had been killed, three wounded, and 33 were missing.

On the day of the attack Second Lieut. Bowitz had been ordered to withdraw from the 10 cm gun which was in a very exposed position at the very end of the Cape Heer headland. When the rearmost destroyer started disembarking troops not far away, Bowitz and a couple of others manned the Oerlikon and fired at them. Then our men came under fire from the "Tirpitz," and her shells started landing uncomfortably close so they were forced to retire, making their way under cover of the smoke up the hill and in as far as Hollenderelva, where they remained until the following day.

Corporal Koren had a shrapnel wound in the leg. He returned next day carried on a stretcher for part of the way, otherwise hobbling along as best he could. I was sent for, but made no attempt to remove the piece of shrapnel, as I did not have the necessary equipment. The wound was bandaged and the leg immobilised and there were subsequently no complications.

On Saturday, 11th September I went to Longyearbyen. At Hotelneset at the entrance to the Adventfjorden, Lieut. Fred Hansteen had been stationed with a 10 cm gun and a crew of ten, as well as smaller guns. On the day of the attack they had been alerted by Longyearbyen, as the man on guard at Hotelneset had fallen asleep at his post. It was then 0235 GMT, and two destroyers were on their way up the fjord. We had had no chance of warning Hotelneset from Barentsburg, as there was no radio contact with them at night.

The ships were flying British colours, and the gun was not manned. Hansteen tried to cope on his own when he realised what was up, but in vain: it was too late. One of the destroyers opened fire just off shore, and there was nothing for it but to clear out. The houses were set on fire, and landing troops destroyed all the equipment and arms, and set off in pursuit. Five of the Norwegians were taken prisoner, while Hansteen and the other five got away.

When the German ships arrived off Longyearbyen they opened fire with an intense cannonade directed at the lower section of the settlement, setting the houses on fire. Then the troops were landed, while the guns raised their sights and demolished the remaining buildings. Local defence consisted of a 40 mm Bofors anti-aircraft gun plus a few smaller pieces, which were no match for the destroyers' 15 cm guns and machine-guns. Captain Trond Vigtel, who was in command, was wounded as he had made his way to the Bofors gun, and was forced to seek cover for a while. When he returned he was hit by a burst of machine-gun fire and killed. The volume of enemy fire had made it difficult to man the other guns which Second Lieuts. Lövaas and Skjelde had tried to fire.

Soon the whole town was in flames, and they had to withdraw in the direction of Sverdrupbyen, closely pursued by the landing troops. Sergeant S. Thorsen kept them at bay for a while with a Bren gun, until he was hit in the head by a bullet which went clean through his helmet and made a gash on the left side of his head, knocking him unconscious. When he came to his senses he lay doggo, and the Germans, assuming he was dead, refrained from taking him prisoner.

He had managed to halt the Germans for a while, giving the others a better chance of withdrawing up the valley to Sverdrupbyen, but they were also harassed by a plane from the battleship "Scharnhorst" which was lying in Adventfjorden. Corporal Trolid fired several bursts at the aircraft but apparently without success.

When the German troops were just short of Sverdrupbyen, they received the signal for withdrawal, and on their way back burnt and destroyed everything still standing. Once they had embarked, the ships aimed several salvos at Sverdrupbyen, setting fire to two houses. At the same time they hit the oil storage tanks on the other side of the fjord at Hjorthamn, which erupted in a sheet of flame and black smoke, as a sort of final farewell.

After the ships had left, all the survivors gathered in Sverdrupbyen; those who had made for the hills came down: 44 men were left, eight were missing. Patrols were sent out to look for them, but without result. It was assumed that they had been taken prisoner. Medical Sergeant T. Kaupang had made a perfect job of sewing Thorsen's wound, and had also managed to salvage some medical supplies in Sverdrupbyen. Everything in Longyearbyen had been destroyed. Captain Vigtel was buried in the local cemetery on 12th September.

Although there was plenty of room in the sickbay in Sverdrupbyen, and rather crowded in Barentsburg, I considered it out of the question to move bed-ridden patients by motor-boat. If we were to encounter a German U-boat en route, our number would be up.

Throughout the entire attack four men were stationed in Sveagruva, blissfully ignorant of what was going on.

M. Thyvold reported that he had been one of the gun-crew manning the Bofors II. The first destroyer withdrew when her bridge started to burn; the destroyer at Finneset fired at the cliff side while troops were being landed, but Bofors II silenced her guns with a number of well-directed hits, but failed to hit the landing craft. Finally only Breidablikk, Nore and he himself were left to man the gun.

A little later when he tried to withdraw from his exposed position at the machine-gun, a German machine-gun fired at him; he replied with a burst, jumped out of his dug-out and literally rolled down the slope. When he reached the Bofors II, he found it abandoned. As he made his way up Sykehus-dalen he was hit by a bullet, and was bandaged by Lieut. Watson, who with his coder was at work blowing up the research station.

The charges went off before Thyvold managed to get clear, and he was knocked unconscious. When he came to, he had been taken prisoner. He had a bullet wound right through his left arm and bits of shrapnel in his head, and was given medical treatment on board one of the destroyers.

The ships reached Bosekopp in Alta on 9th September, and he was admitted to Elvebakken hospital. A. Samuelsen died on board the "Tirpitz," and Flom Jacobsen and W. Palm in Alta. The prisoners included eight wounded, one of them British.

After nearly three weeks they were taken to Narvik and Elvegaardsmoen, where they amused themselves at the expense of Bredsdorff and some of the officers. As there was a shortage of space they were placed in the lock-up reserved for drunks.

The POWs were moved to Trondheim, and from there sent by railway in cattle-trucks to Oslo, where they were confined in Akershus Fort. Thyvold was then shipped on board the notorious "Monte Rosa," which transported Norwegian prisoners to Germany. In Bremen he was placed in solitary confinement, and interrogated over a period of three weeks, but on the whole well treated.

Next stop was Schildberg POW camp in Poland, which had been set up to house Norwegian officers arrested in 1942 and 1943. One of its inmates was General Otto Ruge, GOC during the war in Norway. In 1944 the camp had to be evacuated in face of the Russian advance, and Thyvold and Olseth, another POW from Svalbard managed to make their way to the Russian lines and join a Soviet unit. In March 1945 they passed through Warsaw, which lay in ruins, and with a number of other POWs they reached Scotland via Odessa, where they once more reported for duty at the end of April 1945.

Medical Corporal Kristiansen did a fine job looking after the sick and wounded. He stitched my head wound, proceeding under my directions as I supervised via a mirror.

Despite the misfortunes we had endured, morale was high. On his return to the scene of action, our dentist, an ardent football fan, surveying the burnt-out buildings, declared that the match appeared to have been played mainly in our half. We tried in fact to look on the bright side.

In Barentsburg we now had one Bofors gun to defend ourselves with: all artillery at Hotelneset had been destroyed, while in Longyearbyen the damaged Bofors cannon had been repaired.

With this armament we should be able to keep aircraft and U-boats at arm's length.

When the German ships were first observed in Isfjorden, the radio operator had tried to contact the U.K., but failed to get through. He did, however, send a message to a station in Iceland, which promised to pass it on. Then the Germans started to jam our transmissions. After the conflict our code book was missing, and we assumed that the Germans had taken it, and for this reason we were reluctant to send any messages to the U.K.

Besides, we did not want the Germans to know that the radio station was operative; they probably assumed that it had been destroyed when the research station with its tall masts had been shot to smithereens.

Later we were criticised for maintaining radio silence; but we were not interested in fresh visits by enemy naval vessels, at any rate not for the time being. We were truly on our beam ends, with a number of bed-ridden patients and walking wounded. We had after all alerted Iceland, and the Catalina that circled overhead the day after the attack had quite plainly waggled its wings.

The German ships had sounded the recall signal at 0630 GMT, and as they moved down the fjord we counted eleven vessels in all, two battleships and nine destroyers.

Of our 33 missing men nine badly wounded were treated in the sickbay onboard the "Tirpitz." When Samuelsen died on board his body was consigned to the deep with full naval honours in the presence of a Norwegian and German escort.

According to German records two of the destroyers received two direct hits each from our 10 cm gun, as well as numerous hits from our other armament, and one of them was out of action until 0900 hours GMT, when temporary repairs had been carried out. The third destroyer also received a number of hits. Nine crew members were killed and 49 wounded, while the landing troops had a total of 75 killed.

According to the German naval establishment the nine destroyers represented three flotillas. The three that attacked Barentsburg comprised the 4th flotilla, and included the Z 29, Z 31 and Z 33, making up Landing Force Green. It was the Z 29 that received the first warm welcome from the four-inch cannon, and sustained the greatest damage. The Fifth Flotilla, which attacked Longyearbyen, comprised Landing Force Red, while the Sixth Flotilla was not involved in the attack.

After the Germans had captured the governor and Captain Vigtel had been killed, as a captain I was now the senior officer in Svalbard, representing formally the supreme authority, but as I was not a combatant I handed over day-to-day command to Lieut. Lid. However, we had daily consultations on important matters with the other officers.

The five men killed in Barentsburg were buried on Friday, 10th September. I had previously carried out corpse-inspection, an account of which I attached to my report on the attack, for attention DMS London. The dead were buried with full military honours, and I read the burial service.

Permafrost made it difficult to dig a grave deep and big enough; we had to use hand-granades to break up the soil. It is a well-known fact in Svalbard that after a time the permafrost often disgorges buried bodies.

One of the dead had been shot right through the middle of the heart, by a bullet that had passed through a cigarette packet in his breast pocket. As he had no other wounds it looked uncommonly like an execution. In the heat of warfare mercy killing can only be accepted in the case of personnel wounded beyond hope of recovery.

But this might have been the work of an unusually good German marksman, or a sheer fluke.

After the attack we were without provisions; but reserve depots had previously been deposited in various huts round about, and we were able to fall back on these, one by one. We obtained fresh meat by shooting reindeer and ptarmigan, and we also felled a muskox up in the hills. These animals are by nature endowed with such tough skulls, that these will withstand a rifle bullet, and also such long, thick shaggy hair, that they present a difficult target. When attacked a herd will form a circle, facing outward, with the calves in the middle. They can move at a fast rate, especially uphill, and can be dangerous. Downhill they are at more of a disadvantage, as the forepart of the body is so heavy that they tend to stumble.

During the next few weeks we were frequently "visited" by German planes and U-boats. Early on the morning of 14th September a Ju 88 flew low north along the shore, its engines switched off, but we were ready with our Bofors, and opened fire, whereupon it immediately dived down behind the ridge, switched on its engines, and came into view again further out. It must have been hit, as tracer was seen going straight for it.

Three days later the incident was repeated; every day, in fact, we either saw aircraft or heard the drone of aircraft engines above the clouds, and on 26th September a Heinkel was hit by the gun at Cape Heer.

On 9th October a U-boat surfaced immediately offshore. We opened fire and hit the conning tower, forcing it to dive. This probably prevented the Germans manning their cannon, and blazing away at us, which would have been disastrous, as they would have had no difficulty in blasting everything to smithereens.

Shortly after, the U-boat surfaced, but had to submerge once again when fresh hits were registered. The weather at the time was bad, with sleet and poor visibility. We saw no more of the U-boat, but heard the sound of gunfire out in the fjord, and wondered what it was shooting at, as no shells landed anywhere in the vicinity. We amused ourselves with the theory that it was firing in a fit of fury at having failed to get the better of us.

The following week shots were fired at a U-boat that was spotted twice in Adventfjorden, and this also occurred off Cape Heer.

The volume of U-boat traffic indicated that the Germans had got wind of the arrival of British naval units on their way to evacuate us, and it reached a climax when the British arrived, when the fjord seemed to teem with U-boats.

It was Second Lieut. Breidablikk and his crew who manned the Bofors cannon at Barentsburg, with the same skill as he had shown during the attack, earning no doubt the grudging respect of the enemy.

On 23rd September a Catalina landed just off the quay in Barentsburg, but was forced to take off immediately when a Ju 88 came up Isfjorden. The Catalina landed later at Sveagruva, and landed three men and radio equipment. These reached Barentsburg two days later.

The same day we were visited by another expedition from the U.K. under the command of Captain Roll Lund. There had been speculation as to what had become of us. They arrived onboard "Seadog", the submarine that had fetched us in Signehavn, having left Scapa Flow two weeks earlier, proceeding by day submerged at a speed of only a few knots on their dynamos, and at night on the surface at about ten knots. When they arrived in Isfjorden there were German U-boats in those waters, and "Seadog" had moved off south to Bellsund and on to Sveagruva on 23rd September. From here the expedition had made its way on foot to Barentsburg.

The arrivals told us that the day after the attack a Catalina had been on a flight over Barentsburg and Longyearbyen, but had seen no sign of life. It was the plane we had waved to, and which we assumed had seen us. On the same day a RN submarine had entered the fjord, dodging German U-boats, but had seen no sign of life on land through its periscope. A few days later British naval units had been in these same waters, but the threat posed by U-boats prevented them from approaching close to land.

We too had noticed the increase in the volume of U-boat traffic: the enemy was mobilising for the day when we were to be relieved, and would then strike. That the Germans would be baulked of their prey was another matter.

The expedition included a medical officer, Gunnar Finsen, in the event that I was no longer functioning. I was able to reassure him that everything was under control.

Apart from a bout of food poisoning, which affected the men at Cape Heer, but which soon passed, the general standard of health had been good. A bath had been rigged up in the ruins of the research station, but on the whole the sanitary arrangements were not much to write home about.

A shotgun I had bought in London proved very useful. Ptarmigan were beginning to come down from the hills above Barentsburg, and I

126

bagged quite a number. Our cook proved adept at preparing them; he had also constructed a baking oven in the ruins, which meant fresh bread every day.

Trapping fox was a very popular pastime. Although it was not the best of seasons, we caught a number, kept them caged and waited to be evacuated, as we hoped the fur would fetch a good price in London, where blue fox pelts were in demand.

The question has been raised as to whether the defence of Svalbard had been adequately prepared. No one had foreseen such a massive attack, although we had not dismissed the possibility of a minor operation.

Bredsdorff had applied to London for a bigger defensive force, more guns and an extra wireless operator for Longyearbyen.

Radio contact was made only four times a day between Longyearbyen and Barentsburg, and this was the reason we were unable to warn them when the German ships turned up. But even with only one wireless operator in Longyearbyen contact should have been better and more frequent: we should not have been caught napping. In the circumstances we should have had a look-out post at Reveneset, on the east side of the entrance to Adventfjorden with a good field of vision out Isfjorden, or alternatively at Bjørndalshytta further down the fjord.

The gun emplacements at Cape Heer and Hotelneset were too exposed; had they been better protected and sited a little further back, the guns could have been brought into action when the Germans attacked.

The instructions to the Governor contained a clause to the effect that the garrison "is to protect the Norwegian plant and buildings against enemy activity of limited scope, and prevent lesser enemy forces from taking possession of Svalbard. The garrison on the other hand is not designed to resist a large-scale attack, in which case it is assumed that the military governor will withdraw his forces inland."

Bredsdorff's decision to engage and open fire on a superior enemy force was nevertheless in the circumstances a correct one. Time was too short to undertake an organised withdrawal. We would have been sitting ducks up in the treeless hills, an easy target for superior armed forces and attacks from the air, with only small arms to defend ourselves.

Bredsdorff had also suggested to the authorities in London that the whole garrison should be concentrated in Longyearbyen, leaving only a look-out post at Cape Heer. This would have made it easier to protect Norwegian property. This was agreed on. At the same time coal-mining operations were to be resumed. The Norwegian authorities, with Reksten as their chief spokesman, had succeeded in getting the Admiralty to agree. The coal could either be transported to the U.K. or stored until after the war, when it would be in great demand. An expedition was in fact all set to sail, with reinforcements and equipment, when the Germans struck and put a spoke in the wheel.

Even if the plan had been carried into effect in time, it would have made no real difference, in view of the massive German attack.

We wondered too why the Germans had dispatched such a large fleet to deal with such a small garrison. What did they hope to achieve? Surely not merely the destruction of the radio station and an end to the transmission of weather reports to the Allies? These were admittedly discontinued, but only for two weeks.

Apart from the eleven surface vessels, the Germans had operated with a whole posse of U-boats. While the attack was going forward in Isfjorden it is believed that the battleship "Lützow" with escorting units was in position at the mouth of the fjord, to prevent The Royal Navy from intervening.

Not till after the war did we get a plausible explanation: the attack had been a desperate attempt to justify the presence of the German fleet in the fjords of North Norway. This was to be used against the Allied convoys, but had remained largely inactive. The heavy losses sustained by Convoy PQ 17 in July 1942 were due to insufficient information, and to some extent to the profound respect the Allies had for the battleship "Tirpitz." After the convoy, totalling 34 ships, and crammed with war material, had left Iceland, its departure was reported by German agents. At the same time a Norwegian agent radioed that the "Tirpitz," with a cruiser and escort, had left the Trondheim Fjord and was heading north. It was therefore assumed that they would attack the convoy; but what was not known, was that the "Tirpitz" only proceeded as far as Bogen, near Narvik, and from there the pocket battleships "Admiral Scheer" and "Lützow" had sailed instead.

After the loss of the "Bismarck" in 1941, Hitler was unwilling to risk the sister ship that was superior in size to any Allied vessel, as well as in speed, armament and armour plating, having a displacement of 52,600 tons and a crew of 2530. He feared the aircraft carriers that escorted the convoys. On the other hand the First Sea Lord, Admiral Sir Dudley Pound, was afraid that the "Tirpitz" would prove more than a match for even the largest of the escorting ships. Accordingly on 4th July, when the PQ 17 was north of Finmark, he ordered the convoy to disperse and the escort to withdraw, allowing the convoy to proceed on its own. This gave the German a free hand, and as a result only 11 ships out of the original 34 in the convoy reached their destination. Another reason for this disaster was that the convoy had to sail near the Norwegian coast because of bad ice conditions that year with the ice belt extending further south and it was early in the summer.

The German army, under Field Marshal Dietl, had moved forward from Finmark to attack the Russian northern flank, seize Murmansk, and in this way break this line of supply from the West. In order to ensure adequate protection from seaborne attack, fortifications were erected and naval units sent north, including several battleships, of which the "Tirpitz" was the largest. But Hitler himself had declared that these ships were not to run any unnecessary risk; they were not to proceed so far out to sea that they had no air protection against any Allied carriers escorting the convoys. This meant that they could not attack the convoys as these approached close to Svalbard. The PQ 18 did just that in September. It sailed near the coast of Svalbard, but despite an escort of 40 ships, including a battleship and aircraft-carriers, protecting 39 freighters, 13 of these were lost. The Germans too suffered severe losses, at least 66 airplanes and 7 U-boats.

The reason for this great burst of activity on the part of the Germans so close to Svalbard was that shortly before, Banak in North Norway had not only received an extra squadron of reconnaissance planes but had also been made the base for an entire group of FW 200 bomber planes. At the same time Bardufoss had been made a base for torpedo bombers, the most effective weapon against ships. These bombers attacked the convoy flying low and very fast, 42 of them, in a long line abreast, dropping their torpedoes and going into a barrage of fire from the escorts. The next day in a similar attack they suffered a total loss of 33 planes. Both days there ensued an intense fight, the bomber planes dropping their load and the destroyers from the escort hunting the U-boats.

After the disaster PQ 17 Bomber Command had transferred several squadrons to North Russia to protect the convoys.

Following this great battle at sea the activity of the Germans against the convoys was greatly reduced.

RAF Bomber Command made great efforts to cripple torpedo production in Germany, and the idea was also conceived of countering torpedo attacks on Allied convoys by sabotaging the torpedo storage plant in North Norway. A commando unit consisting of British, Canadian and Norwegian personnel was raised under the leadership of Lieut.-Commander A. R. Glen and trained in the Cairngorms in Scotland. They were due to be flown by a Catalina in January 1943 to Revsbotn in Finnmark, and from there make their way to Banak, and after completing their task cross over into Sweden. It had been wrongly assumed that the torpedo bombers took off from Banak, and not from Bardufoss. With the landing of the Americans in North Africa, however, the torpedo bombers were sent south, and the plan was abandoned.

Some six months before the attack on Svalbard the German ships had sailed out to strike at a convoy, but had withdrawn in face of a powerful escort force. Hitler was furious with Admiral Räder, who resigned, and despite Hitler's apology remained adamant. He was replaced by Admiral Dönitz.

When things started to go badly for the Germans on the east front, Dönitz was told that the naval units in the north would have to play a more active role in the battle against the convoys, so as to prevent vital supplies from reaching the Soviet Union. If they failed in good time to produce results the ships would be called back to Germany, the units dissolved, and the crews sent to the Russian front. Faced with this threat the German navy decided to strike at Svalbard. The operation was led by Admiral Kummetz, who had been in command of the battle cruiser "Blücher" when she was sunk in Oslo Fjord on 9th April, 1940, the day the Germans invaded Norway. The "Blücher" went down with most of her crew, but Kummetz managed to swim ashore.

The German reports that were issued after the attack were grossly exaggerated, listing the destruction of large-scale military installations, ammunition dumps and oil storage-tanks, as well as the blowing-up of weather reporting stations, all of which was intended to impress Hitler. The mention of a large number of German dead and wounded merely served to enhance this effect.

The first convoy sailed to Russia in August 1941 and for the rest of the year convoys to Russia continued to run with fair regularity without any loss of ships. However, in January the Germans started to attack the convoys and ships were lost. More protection was needed; the escorts were increased and bigger ships used as cover. In the beginning of March 1942 the "Tirpitz" took part in an attack on a convoy and she just missed being hit by torpedoes when she was attacked by a destroyer and a plane from a British carrier. She immediately took refuge in Narvik and didn't take part in further attacks on convoys.

At the end of March the PQ 14 was met by combined German forces east of Bear Island and 5 out of 19 ships were lost.

No convoys were sent to Russia between September and December owing to the landing in North Africa, but 37 independent sailings took place, of which 28 arrived at their destination.

However, on 31st December, 1942 a memorable battle was fought in the north when British naval forces successfully defended a convoy against superior German forces without any cargo ship being lost. A force of 5 destroyers attacked the German cruiser "Admiral Hipper" and the pocket battleship "Lützow" in addition to six German destroyers. In the end when the British Cruisers "Sheffield" and "Jamaica" arrived the Germans had to withdraw. The leader of the attack, Captain Sherbrook R.N. on H.M.S. "Onslow" was wounded when his ship received several hits and he got his V.C.

In January and February 1943 convoys left from Loch Ewe in Scotland and were attacked at Bear island and Iceland, but all ships arrived safely in Russia. The first convoy lost a ship on the return voyage. The second convoy met strong gales and many cargo ships had to return, but no ships were lost.

Because of the heavy losses in the summer of 1942, much of it due to continuous daylight, no convoys were sent between March and October 1943. However, ships and destroyers proceeded independently. In October when more ships were available after the landing in Italy the convoys to Russia were resumed, and for the rest of the year no ships were lost.

Until the end of the war convoys to Russia continued to be attacked by the Germans except for the summer of 1944 when no convoys were sent owing to the invasion in Normandy.

As more units allocated for escort duty, losses decreased. However, the Germans were not the only enemy to be overcome but the violent winter gales.

In all, 41 convoys were sent from the U.K. to Russia with a total loss of 2580 lives. About 80 Allied merchant ships were sunk and 19 units from the R.N.

The shots fired by the "Tirpitz" against Barentsburg marked her swansong. Fourteen days later, in Kaafjord, North Norway, she was mortally wounded when British commandos in one-man subs placed limpet mines on her hull, killing 40 and inflicting so much damage that she was put out of action for several months. The "Scharnhorst" suffered an almost similar fate, but on the day that the "Tirpitz" was mined, the "Scharnhorst" was carrying out target practice, as her shooting during the attack on Longyearbyen had proved highly inaccurate. This provided some respite, but on Christmas Day in 1943 the "Scharnhorst" was sunk in the Barents Sea by an Allied naval force in which the Norwegian destroyer "Stord" played a notable part.

In December 1943 an Allied convoy on its way to Murmansk was spotted by German planes, which observed that the escort consisted only of minor warships. This news prompts the "Scharnhorst" to leave harbour accompanied by four destroyers. When a storm blows up the destroyers are ordered back to port. What the German spotter planes had not seen was that a large British squadron had been waiting in the background. It included the Norwegian destroyer "Stord," and was commanded by Admiral Sir Bruce Fraser, who had hoisted his flag in the battleship "Duke of York." The Allied ships closed in on the "Scharnhorst," cutting off her retreat. Admiral Bey decides to fight it out, and orders his crew to fight to the bitter end for the honour of Germany. Direct hits fired from the "Duke of York's" powerful guns considerably reduce the "Scharnhorst's" speed, and she is soon an easy prey to her numerically superior foe, but Admiral Bey refuses to give in. Several torpedoes strike home, and the "Stord," too, scores a hit. Soon the "Scharnhorst" goes to her watery grave, taking her entire crew with her, providing a dramatic sight for the Allied crews who watch her sink, many with bared heads in honour of the 1800 who are forced to sacrifice their lives to the misguided pride of an admiral.

The "Tirpitz" was attacked once more on the 3rd April, 1944 as she lay in Altafjorden, this time by RAF carrier bombers. Although protected by torpedo nets her superstructure was completely razed, and finally on 12th November, 1944, she was sunk west of Tromsø, another RAF Bomber Command feat. At 1000 hours on 19th October the first British destroyer sailed up Isfjorden, closely followed by a cruiser and three more destroyers, one of which changed course and made for Barentsburg, while the others continued up the fjord.

We immediately carried our personal belongings down to the quay, and Nore, with his head wound, was brought down on a specially designed stretcher with an attached vest, which made it possible for him to be transported at all sorts of angles. This proved very useful when he had to be transferred from the motor launch to the deck of the destroyer.

At 1330 hours the destroyer "Onslaught" hove to a short distance off shore. It was important to retain freedom of movement in case a U-boat should turn up. Motorboats were launched which came ashore to pick us up, and in less than an hour we had all been embarked, after which we set off at full speed down Grönnfjorden and up Isfjorden. In Adventfjorden we were to join the other ships that were embarking people in Longyearbyen and putting new personnel ashore. No one was landed in Barentsburg, as there were inadequate housing facilities there.

Once on board, we were invited to a cup of tea in the wardroom. Hardly had we enjoyed the taste of the beverage than we heard a terrific crash that shook the whole ship. A torpedo, I thought.

Everyone rushed on deck, but the ship continued on her course seemingly unharmed, though at somewhat reduced speed. On the bridge I was informed that we had collided with a U-boat, which was just about to surface. The U-boat had been registered on the asdic, but had been taken for one of the large ice-floes drifting in the fjord.

We saw no trace of the U-boat. Had it gone to the bottom? Later we intercepted SOS signals from it, so it must have been severely damaged.

The destroyer had damaged one propeller, reducing her speed, as we noticed when we reached Adventfjorden where several U-boats had been detected. These were being hunted with depth-charges, and great columns of water rose from the surface. We joined in the chase, but owing to our reduced speed our depth-charges exploded uncomfortably close, shaking the whole ship. It would start with a strange vibration on the water surface, which would then seethe and bubble and rear up in a great column of spray.

It is not advisable to fall overboard when this is going on and depth-charges are exploding. The shock wave in the water will cause internal bleeding and intestinal rupture, with the contents of bowels erupting into abdomen and inducing highly dangerous peritonitis. Quite a number of persons died in this way during the war at sea, and I have personally dealt with this in an article in a medical journal.

While we were busily engaged at the entrance to the Advent Fjord, the other destroyers were engaged further up in protecting the cruiser, which was embarking personnel to be evacuated and putting new personnel ashore.

The idea had been for us to be transferred to the cruiser as well, but in view of the situation we remained onboard the destroyer, as it was vital for the cruiser to make her getaway as rapidly as possible, in view of the threat of a torpedo attack.

We must have presented a tempting target to the German U-boats: one American cruiser and one destroyer plus three British destroyers. But the Germans undoubtedly had their hands full escaping all the exploding depth-charges.

As soon as everyone was safely on board, we set off at full speed down Isfjorden. As we passed Grönnfjorden, we had our last glimpse of Barentsburg, where we had spent close on five exciting months, and which had now been transformed into a mass of charred ruins and still smoking heaps of coal.

As we could only do 13 knots, we were soon left well astern; the other ships had soon disappeared over the horizon, while Svalbard's peaks and glaciers sank down in the east.

We had an uneventful voyage to Seydisfjord on the east coast of Iceland, arriving in the morning of 22nd October to find the other ships at anchor waiting for us.

We were now transferred to the US cruiser "Tuscaloosa," a so-called heavy cruiser of about 10,000 tons. In August 1941 she had brought President Roosevelt to New Foundland for his historic meeting with Winston Churchill, when the Atlantic Charter was signed. Churchill arrived in the battleship "Prince of Wales," which not long before had played her role in the sinking of the "Bismarck," Germany's powerful battleship, which would have wreaked havoc on Allied convoys if she had reached the Atlantic unscathed.

Our four wounded were taken good care of in the ship's sickbay, and all in all we had a pleasant crossing to Scotland in the company of our genial and hospitable hosts.

Three days later, on 25th October, we docked in Greenock, from where the wounded were sent to Craiglockhart, the Norwegian hospital in Edinburgh for further treatment; while the other members of the expedition returned to their respective units. I took the train to London to submit my report to the DMS.

Hospital in Scotland

In the late autumn of 1943 I was appointed head of the Brigade hospital. The Norwegian Brigade had now been moved to Callander in Perthshire, north of Edinburgh, where three companies and Brigade H.Q. were posted. The hospital had been set up in Lendrick Lodge, a property a few miles west of the town. The house itself was large enough for its purpose, and contained wards as well as an operating theatre, which enabled me to carry out minor operations, such as removing the occasional troublesome appendix.

A range of hills to the north provided the mountain companies, on which the Brigade was now based, with fine training facilities, under somewhat primitive conditions at Dal Camp, though this was of course an essential part of the whole programme.

In company with Brigade M.O. Helge Kraft-Strøm I visited the camp, where one of the company commanders had been nick-named Tarzan, as he spent much of his time running round the hills with his men. The Brigade Commander was colonel Hans Holtermann.

The training section was located on the east coast, in St. Andrews, not least celebrated for its golf courses, and was the scene throughout 1944 of intense planning for the day when Norway would be liberated, such as the setting up of regional commands. These courses were attended not only by officers from the various units in the Brigade, but also by many from the London offices of the Norwegian High Command. I attended some myself.

Various sporting activities were also organised for the troops, including football matches with local Scots, in which the Norwegians acquitted themselves creditably.

Just west of Callander were the Trossachs with a well-known resort hotel near a large lake, where a grand party was organised on New Year's Eve, at which the Scots performed their national dances with great gusto. We Norwegians also had a go, but our Terpsichorean achievements were hardly worthy of public exhibition.

In April the Brigade hospital was moved to Cupar, not far from St Andrews, where we were also able to serve the needs of the Norwegian Navy's air and sea base at Woodhaven near Dundee. We were also close to Leuchars, the RAF station to which many Norwegians were flown from Sweden. In 1944 Colonel Balchen was entrusted with the task of starting this valuable shuttle service between Sweden and Scotland, which was operated mainly by American aircraft and crews, and provided a vital link with Scandinavia for the rest of the war.

Serving with the British—
Preparing for Invasion

On Tuesday, 12th September, 1944, I took the night train to London. I had been called to a conference with the DMS, at which I was asked if I would like to be attached to a British field ambulance which was stationed in Lincolnshire. The answer was Yes.

For security reasons I was not told what plans were in store for the field ambulance.

I took the train to Lincoln, a city renowned for its magnificent cathedral, and boarded a local train to Candelsby, and from there went by car to Horncastle, a few miles inland from the east coast. On the last stretch of my journey I passed numerous military encampments and airfields all buzzing with activity. I realised that something was brewing.

When I arrived another Norwegian doctor was leaving. Although he was in uniform I assumed that he was from the Medical Directorate, and probably had some idea of what was afoot.

The field ambulance turned out to be the one to which I had been attached for three weeks in Scotland in the early part of 1943, when it had been stationed at Rothes, a village in the heart of the Scottish Highlands, west of Aberdeen. It comprised the medical unit of one of the battalions of the 52nd Lowland Division, which was stationed in the surrounding country.

Other Norwegian officers had also been attached to the division, which was then organised and equipped as a mountain division, intended for operations in Norway, and was amply supplied with the appropriate arms and material. During those three weeks I had enjoyed the opportunity of walking in the hills during our divisional manœuvres.

Rothes was a pleasant village, with no less than seven whisky distilleries, and one might have expected that the mess would have been well stocked with the local product, but no such luck. It was all destined for the export market, where it earned Britain much-needed hard currency. Our own meagre whisky rations had come from Edinburgh.

One remarkable feature of the village was that most of the children were red-haired and freckled, reminding me of the inhabitants of certain villages in West Norway.

My stay in Rothes had coincided with Robert Burn's birthday, 30th January, one of Scotland's great national festivals, traditionally celebrated with the eating of haggis, a dish with which we were not familiar, but went down well, assisted by the national drink.

It was a pleasure to meet my old colleagues from the field ambulance. There were ten of them, and the set-up was undoubtedly a trifle peculiar: the officer in command was a lieutenant-colonel who had seen service in the Western Desert, a somewhat incompetent individual who was frequently being corrected by his subordinates, in particular a hot-tempered little supply officer who openly dressed him down on several occasions. But fortunately he had an efficient second-in-command who usually managed to sort things out. He had spent some time climbing in the Himalayas.

The task now assigned to the Division was quite different from the one for which it had been training in Scotland. It was to provide the reserve force for the airborne attack on Arnheim, and would be deployed if the operation proved a success. It would be transported by plane and towed glider. The field ambulance was conveyed on jeeps, which would be driven onboard the planes. One jeep would be able to transport up to four stretchers. We practised stowing our equipment on jeeps, and driving them in and out of gliders.

Although the Division was designated the 52nd Lowland Division, which would indicate that its troops were Scottish, this was not the case. The ranks included some Scots, but the majority were from England, especially Yorkshire, the latter speaking a dialect which I often found difficult to understand. This sometimes created problems when I was out on a training exercise and was in charge. Usually my sergeant dealt with the men, but he was not always willing to help me out, and as a result I frequently committed a faux pas, which he would gleefully recount to the C.O. when we returned to camp.

Morale in our unit was not of the best: for several years its members had been training, day in, day out, always the same unvarying routine. Every third month they were entitled to the regular week's leave, but this hardly provided the right sort of break. They were all impatient to see active service.

To a certain extent tea helped to keep our spirits up. It came round in large urns five times a day to every mess. It was brewed in these urns, and mixed with milk and sugar to produce a delightful beverage. The men would queue up at these tea-breaks, all with their half-litre mugs, and their spirits would rise noticeably as the warm liquid went down. In many ways the general mood was expressed in racy language and bawdy turns of phrase.

A few miles to the east of us lay the seaside town of Skegness, where a number of large hotels had been requisitioned by the RAF, and halfway between Horncastle and Skegness was a small village, where a Norwegian lady, the widow of a well-known British World War One general, lived. Via the jungle telegraph she got to know that there was a Norwegian Officer in the neighbourhood, and in due course I received an invitation to her home. Apparently despite efforts to conceal the activities of our division, security was not particularly watertight.

The Arnhem operation, with airborne troops landed behind enemy lines in Holland, was launched on 17th September, 1944, and proved a grievous defeat for the Allies. The Germans had prior warning of the attack, and had concentrated troops and armour in the threatened area. Allied intelligence was aware of this enemy build-up, and passed on the information. It is not known with complete certainty whether this report failed to reach the Supreme Command, or whether it was disregarded. A tremendous amount of preparatory work had been undertaken in planning this operation, and a large number of troops and a great deal of equipment made available, which may have been an important reason why it was actually launched.

We were no longer required as a reserve force for the airborne troops, and plans were now altered. It was decided that we were to travel by train and boat to the front in Holland and Belgium. Judging by what we were subsequently told, we were lucky not to have arrived by glider, as this appears to have been a rather risky business.

The Germans were the first to land troops by glider during the invasion of Crete, when so many mishaps, involving loss of life, occurred, that they never repeated the experiment. On that occasion the landing zone was mountainous, and a great many transports crashed. This was the main reason for the disastrous results. During the invasion of Sicily in September 1943 the British used gliders, and this time too the landing zone was mountainous. The operation was poorly planned and ill prepared, and the consequent loss of life and equipment amounted to little short of a disaster, as only a fraction of the glider-borne troops went into action, and many of the planes fell in the sea or crashed in the rugged terrain. Fully laden jeeps and guns in many cases were hurled forward on impact, crushing accompanying troops.

Technically the air-drop at Arnhem proved more successful, as a great many troops were landed, but here too many accidents occurred and a large number killed. The crossing of the Rhine by glider-borne troops was more of a success, a large number of men being brought across.

The Landing on Walcheren

On Tuesday, 17th October, we were on our way south in a troop-train crammed with men and equipment. As all mainline tracks lead to London, we would have to pass through the capital. As a rule one always has to de-train at any one of London's terminals, and proceed to another station in another part of the town, but for security reasons we were not allowed to leave the train, which went halfway round London, passing one station after another, and being shunted from siding to siding, in fits and starts. After many boring hours we reached the south side of town, and were now able to continue on our journey on the Southampton line.

In the evening we reached Gosport on the south coast, where we were installed in an old fort by the name of Monckton, situated on a small promontory at the entrance to Southampton harbour, just across the water from the Isle of Wight.

Two days later we embarked in the "Princess Astrid" in Southampton, and the following day we put to sea.

After a calm and pleasant crossing of the Channel we landed at Ostend the following day without incident, and were quartered in what had been a German barrack. In the week that followed we were stationed in various parts of north-west Belgium, where we realised some sort of action was being planned. On Friday, 27th October we attended a conference at divisional H.Q. in Ansegham, where we were briefed on the forthcoming operations.

On Tuesday, 31st October we made our way to Berskens, a town on the south side of the Scheldt estuary, an important stepping-stone on the road to Antwerp. The British had already taken Antwerp on 4th September, and it was now vital to gain control of the northern bank of the river, so that a more direct supply route could be opened up to the combat zone, thus avoiding the long roundabout route from Normandy. The Germans were established in considerable strength on the north bank of the river, both on Walcheren and the Zeeland peninsula on the landward side. The division's task was to cross the river and dislodge the enemy. Our first objective was the town of Flushing (Flemish: Vlissingen) on the island of Walcheren, situated 5 kilometres across the water immediately opposite Breskens.

At night an intense artillery bombardment opened up from the south bank, under cover of which British commandos crossed in landing craft and amphibian tanks moving downstream, and establishing a bridge-head on the outskirts of Flushing. We followed on their heels in a landing craft, at dawn. German artillery had opened up, and a veritable firework display lit up the sky above.

We landed safely on the river bank in the town and set up a temporary aid post just above, but soon moved into the centre of town, where we established an ADS (Advanced Dressing Station) in an engineering workshop, a short distance from a large crane. Inside the driver's cabin, high above the ground, a German started taking pot-shots at us, but without registering a hit. Well protected by his iron "cage", he seemed immune to attack, but suddenly silence descended. He had either been killed or had run out of ammunition.

After a while a steadily increasing stream of dead and wounded was brought in by stretcher-bearers either on stretchers or on jeeps equipped with brackets for two stretchers. Small amphibian vehicles, Weasels, were also used, as there was considerable flooding after the dikes had been breached.

The stretcher-bearers had provided first aid in the field, applying dressings to wounds, staunching serious bleeding, if necessary by applying a tourniquet to an arm or a leg. After a case had been registered wounds and other injuries were treated, fractures immobilised and intravenous infusions given.

Minor cases could be sent back to their units, but in serious cases requiring an operation and further treatment, the wounded were sent to the divisional field hospital in the rear areas. In our case this meant being conveyed down to the beach by jeep, and crossing the Scheldt by boat to ambulances waiting on the other side, and thence on to the field hospital. If long-term treatment was envisaged, cases would be sent to a base hospital.

The medical officers at the ADS were allotted various tasks. I was to be in charge of the so-called surgical department, as I had rather more experience of this than the others. Our work consisted mainly of treating wounds, cleaning them, and sewing the necessary stitches.

As a rule there was not much one could do with bullet wounds, where the exit aperture was bigger than that of entry. Shrapnel wounds were larger, but the worst wounds were those caused by landmines, which the enemy had planted in great numbers, and which accounted for many fatalities. Those who survived suffered fearsome injuries with gaping wounds and broken bones.

Many of the dead and wounded had been hit by their own guns firing from the south bank. To assist an infantry advance the artillery are supposed to lay down a barrage to cover the ground ahead of the infantry, and lift this carpet of fire as the foot soldiers move forward. The success of this depends on co-operation between the gunners and their observation posts, and of course in any advance through a town this is difficult. In addition our artillery was operating a good way behind the front line.

Major operations are not supposed to be carried out at first aid posts, which are not equipped for them. But occasionally one is forced to do so. One case involved a soldier who had stepped on a landmine; the whole of his calf had been smashed. His leg below the knee was a great gaping wound with bone splinters all higgledy-piggledy. A tourniquet had been applied to his thigh, but this had failed to stop the bleeding completely. He was in a pretty bad way, and had lost a lot of blood.

The C.O. was not present, but after conferring with few of the other doctors we decided that the situation was so critical that we should have to amputate at the knee.

I used an ordinary surgeon's scalpel, applied ligatures to the arteries and also the sciatic nerve to prevent the patient feeling the actual incision of it. He had been given a dose of morphine and reacted less strongly than might have been expected. Later on I was told that he had made a good recovery, and an amputation low on the thigh had been correctly executed.

Afterwards I was criticised, and told that amputations should not be carried out at an ADS (Advanced Dressing Station), but those who were not there at the time had no means of judging the situation. As fighting continued more dead were brought in than we could manage to send on, and they were therefore stacked outside the post, each one with a label tied to his foot. They were young men in the bloom of youth, tanned and in splendid physical shape when death struck. What a waste of human life—an impression heightened by the very heap of bodies.

Bit by bit the Germans were driven out of the town, and retreated to the north. When the battle for the town was over, we transferred our station to the northern outskirts, where the Germans had built a hospital inside a bombproof shelter.

Walcheren had been simultaneously attacked from the seaward side to the west, at Westkapelle, after the dikes had been breached by aerial bombardment. The ground had been flooded to force the Germans to pull out their troops. Walcheren was literally one vast fortress, manned by numerous well-trained troops intent on preventing the Allies from using Antwerp as a port for supplying their armies.

The fortifications had also been pounded by the guns of Allied naval units in an attempt to silence the German artillery, but their gun emplacements were bomb-proof, and gave the landing troops some unpleasant surprises.

Early on the morning of 1st November, Royal Marines, reinforced by British, Canadian, Belgian and Norwegian commandos, were on their way north along the coast from Ostend, where they had been training. They arrived in large landing-craft filled with amphibian vehicles where the troops sat, ready to drive ashore. The Norwegian contingent amounted to over 100 men, in two landing-craft. As they approached Walcheren a veritable armada of Allied warships came steaming in from the open sea to the west, with orders to remain in the background and provide artillery support during the landing operations. Low cloud-cover precluded any air support.

The landing-craft turn in the direction of Westkapelle, where the dyke had been breached by gunfire for a distance of a few hundred yards, and as they move in they wait expectantly for the Germans to open fire. But they bide their time, and a few salvos from the warships fail to provoke any reaction from the shore.

Just as the landing crafts are close to the beach and the troops are about to go ashore the Germans open up with a lethal rain of machine-gun fire and mortar shells. Mines attached to stakes in the seabottom explode on impact; direct hits are scored on rocket-launching craft which disintegrate with a roar. Most of the landing crafts are sunk or destroyed, and many of the tanks go down. Troops try to swim or wade ashore, and make their way up the beach, but many are killed, and the offshore waters are soon strewn with dead bodies. Some, however, reach the comparative safety of the dike, where they are screened from small arms fire, and make for the breach.

After a while the weather improved, making air support possible, with Norwegian squadrons playing their part, and meanwhile more and more men managed to get ashore in their amphibian tanks—so-called Buffaloes and Weasels—and scrambled unharmed up the beach.

After pouring through the breach and overcoming enemy resistance, British commandos moved south on the road to Flushing to link up with the commandos that had crossed the Scheldt at the spot where we had landed.

The Norwegian contingent was not involved in the first wave, and came through relatively unscathed, but after landing they helped to take the towns of Westkapelle and Domburg further north, and in this phase their casualties were four dead and seventeen wounded.

In mid-January 1945 they also participated in the attempted crossing of the Maas, where five were killed, including B. Myrvaag, who had been present during the German attack of 8th September, 1943, in Svalbard.

In planning the attack on Westkapelle timing was vital, owing to the great difference between high and low tide. The sand dunes meant that landing-craft could only get ashore at certain hours of the day and days of the month. Tidal differences would also decide whether the stakes on the sea bottom were struck and the mines exploded.

The Norwegian Air Force taking part in the Walcheren campaign also suffered a number of losses, but continued to play their part in the Allied advance.

On Day Five the Germans surrendered officially. This took place in Middelburg, in the centre of Walcheren, and was the result more or less of an inspired bluff, when a British officer and his Norwegian colleague managed to persuade the German Commandant that they had far more numerous forces at their disposal than was actually the case.

But this did not mean that fighting was at an end: the enemy was entrenched behind a strong fortification in the north-west corner of the island which held out until Day 8, after considerable loss of life.

The Walcheren landings comprise one of the bloodiest operations on the western front. Thousands of young men went straight to their death, and the heavy losses in British lives at Walcheren came as a great shock to the British public. The Germans had been really well prepared, and showed great resourcefulness.

With some of the wounded we made our way up the canal by boat to Middelburg, partly driving on the dikes running along the canal with flooded country on both sides. Middelburg, an interesting medieval town, with a cathedral and many other beautiful buildings, is regarded as the capital of the island. It had suffered little damage, and now stood on a rise in the middle of the floods.

Most of the German troops had succeeded in crossing the dike into South Beverland, and making their way across a narrow strip of land to the mainland, to the immediate north of Antwerp. Montgomery was subsequently criticised for not trying to stop the enemy here, and he also had to put up with further criticism for not taking the necessary steps to drive the Germans from the area round the Scheldt, which would have opened up a supply route via Antwerp at an earlier date.

Montgomery had been repeatedly urged to do this by Eisenhower, and even Churchill had pressed him to do so, but Montgomery was somewhat reluctant to take orders. It was not until Eisenhower sent him a sharp letter containing a veiled ultimatum that he yielded. Not before the middle of October did he launch an offensive on the south bank of the Scheldt with American and Canadian troops. Later he admitted that he had made a mistake in waiting so long. The task of opening up the Scheldt was not completed before the Germans had been driven from Walcheren, at a cost to the Allies of 13,000 killed and wounded.

Montgomery's dilatoriness gave the enemy time to mine the river, and valuable time was lost in making it safe for shipping.

The long supply lines from Cherbourg in Normandy meant a shortage of materials and fuel for vehicles, artillery and tanks, and pursuit of the retreating enemy ground to a halt, giving the Germans time to rally for the Ardennes counter-offensive in December.

As already mentioned many of the dead whose bodies were brought in to the aid post in Flushing had been killed by their own artillery. The same fate had befallen U.S. troops in July 1944 attempting to break out from their bridgeheads against stiff German resistance. In appalling weather conditions American planes dropped their bombs on their own troops, killing and wounding large numbers. (It is usually estimated that there is one killed to every two wounded.) Two bomber groups in particular "distinguished" themselves by bombing their own forces, and what is more, on more than one occasion, for which reason they were dubbed "Die Luftwaffe." The real Luftwaffe, heavily outnumbered, hardly put in an appearance. The bad weather that persisted at the start of the invasion greatly reduced the efficiency of air support, and proved a great advantage to the enemy.

The RAF, too, bombed their own troops: during the Canadian advance on Falaise in the middle of August, aimed at closing the trap on a pocket of German resistance, about one hundred Allied troops were killed by RAF bombs and many more wounded.

General Patton was at the time on his way north to pin the Germans down at Falaise, having broken out with his Third Army from the Normandy bridgehead, and turned south and east towards Argentan. On his way north to close the trap he was ordered by Eisenhower to stop; Montgomery would deal with that problem. Furious protest from Patton proved unavailing. Unfortunately Montgomery's Canadian divisions failed to arrive in time, and most of the Germans got away. It has been estimated that there were between 50 and 100 thousand of them in the pocket at the time.

Eisenhower was apt to pay more attention to Montgomery than to his own generals, as Patton discovered. The German troops who got away before the trap could be sprung at Falaise were later deployed elsewhere, e.g. in the Ardennes.

Ironically the troops Montgomery had failed to put in the bag in August, turned up again in September. When Monty's parachute force dropped round Arnhem there were two German panzer divisions, that had broken out at Falaise, to meet them.

The Ardenne offensive came as a complete surprise to the Allies. The Ultra intelligence team had managed to break the German radio code, and intercepted messages suggested that a counter-offensive was planned, but for several reasons these were not trusted. As an extra precaution, in preparing their attack, the Germans made use of telephonic rather than wireless communication.

For this reason the messages were somewhat vague and unsubstantiated, and were not given sufficient credence. Besides, Hitler had his hands full on the eastern front, and the Germans were assumed to be retreating on every battlefield. The Allied Commanders were beginning to feel that they had the situation under control, and that the war on the western front had almost been won.

With this attack the Allied position rapidly took a turn for the worse. At first they were forced to give ground, fighting in snow and cold against a powerful German thrust that was launched in the middle of December. Gradually the Germans were pushed back, although at one time the situation was critical. The Allied command was waiting impatiently for the fresh Soviet offensive planned just east of Warsaw, but this was delayed.

Soviet forces had advanced as far as the Polish capital, but waited for a while before moving in, allegedly to give the Germans time to crush the resistance fighters in the city who had become increasingly active as the Russians approached. The Poles, alas, were unaware of Soviet intentions, and were confident that liberation was just round the corner.

Finally in January the Russian armies that had halted just short of Warsaw launched their attack, and this meant that pressure on the Allies in the west eased.

The delay in opening up Antwerp as a supply harbour was to have a considerable bearing on the further progress of the war. Had it occurred earlier the Allied advance could have continued unimpeded, and the enemy would in all probability not have been in a position to launch a counter-offensive. General Patton, with his Third Army, could then have struck at the heart of Germany, and given Hitler the shock of his life. Thanks to his achievements in Sicily and more recently on the western front, Patton was the man der Führer feared most of all. Admittedly Patton was to some extent being held back by Eisenhower, who held the view that the best strategy was to advance on a broad front, and disapproved of Patton's highly individual thrusts, even though these had so far produced brilliant results. To some extent Patton had the support of his immediate superior, General Omar Bradley, but the latter was bound to defer to Eisenhower. Montgomery, who for some time had been making comparatively little progress, shared Eisenhower's view.

Eisenhower's treatment of Patton was due in part to their personal relations, which were not of the best. This was partly due to the much-publicised blunder Patton had committed in Sicily, when during a visit to a military hospital he had struck a patient suffering from so-called shell-shock, but which he put down to malingering. The incident was widely reported in the American press, and a great many people were clamouring for Patton's head.

As a result he was given no higher command during the remainder of the Italian campaign, nor at the start of the Normandy invasion. It was only when the advance started to bog down that he was given a free rein.

It was in fact a medical problem that called a temporary halt to Patton's career, with dire consequences for the further progress of the war.

When he was finally given command of the Third Army in Normandy this was kept secret, so as to ensure that Hitler would not concentrate troops on his sector of the front. For a while his victories were made public without Patton's name being mentioned; this greatly annoyed him, as he was keen to be rehabilitated.

As Supreme Commander Eisenhower had a difficult task getting American and British generals to co-operate. Relations were often strained. Montgomery, who commanded the British land forces, found it difficult to toe the line under Eisenhower, at times sabotaging orders from above, and coming within an ace of being dismissed from his post. But as a rule Eisenhower did his best to iron out these differences, even though in doing so he tended to give Montgomery the benefit of the doubt, rather than his own generals, especially in matters of supply and strategic questions, for example when he placed American troops under Montgomery's command. The Americans considered that he was unduly passive, with a view to saving his own troops, but his major blunder, in their eyes, was the delay in opening up the supply route through Antwerp, with the dire consequences this entailed.

Mistakes made by incompetent generals may result in wholesale loss of human life, an appalling fact that unfortunately has to be accepted in war, and is the inevitable consequence of human failure. Eisenhower was not slow to dismiss generals who failed to come up to the mark.

It has been maintained that the war on the western front would have ended several months sooner, had the supply of fuel continued uninterrupted. The delay in opening up Antwerp as a supply harbour was an important reason for the hold-up.

On Tuesday 14th November we re-crossed the Scheldt in a large landing-craft which had ferried tanks and artillery across. We continued through Ghent and Antwerp to Bergen op Zoom, where we made a temporary halt. Antwerp had now become a military staging post and the most important supply harbour for the Allies on the western front, and for this reason it attracted the special attention of the Germans, who launched swarms of V2 rockets on the town. These exploded all around, just as in London.

The streets were teeming with service personnel, many on short leave from the front.

After a short while we moved to 's Hertogenbosch, where we were billetted in a school. We were now close to the German lines, and could see V2 rockets being launched on their way to England, mounting vertically before attaining their curved trajectory, and trailing a tail of fire.

The town, which had suffered little war damage, was dominated by a beautiful cathedral. We were invited to the home of a local doctor, who gave us an account of conditions under the Germans—essentially the same as in Norway.

At the end of November I was recalled to London. I went by jeep to Antwerp, where the Military Police requisitioned our car, whose driver had to foot it back to his unit. From there I obtained transport to a transit camp in Ostend, and next day reached Southampton by boat, arriving in London on the following day.

At a Base Hospital in Brussels

In December I took part in a course of war-surgery at Hammersmith Hospital, thanks to my attachment to a British army hospital in Belgium, and in the middle of January I flew to Brussels.

I had been posted to L'Hôpital Bruggmann, the town's main hospital, situated on the outskirts of the capital and now serving as a base hospital. It was a modern establishment housed in several buildings and pavilions.

The orthopaedic ward where I started consisted almost entirely of two large rooms, one for knee injuries and one for ankle injuries. We were actually not treating war wounds, but injuries incurred out in the open on exercises or in the pursuit of sport. Football was an important leisure occupation for troops out of the firing line, and helped to keep them in good physical shape.

We had to deal with a great many knee-cartilage cases; these were operated on using a much easier technique than the one I had learnt. It was highly important that exercise and movement should be started as early as the day after the operation.

There were many cases of sprained ankles, and I had to revise my ideas on how to treat them. There was no question here of immobilising the affected limb with an elastic bandage. Provided no ligaments had been severely damaged, exercise and massage were started as soon as the patient had been admitted. Although this might at first provoke a certain amount of moaning and groaning, it was astonishing to see how quickly patients recovered. Elastic bandages are nevertheless useful in treating walking cases, for patients not confined to bed, but they must be removed when resting, so as to enable the joint to be exercised. Exercise at an early stage was also the rule for simple knee injuries, such as the frequent incidences of water on the knee, which is an inflammation without infection.

The object was to get patients back to their units as quickly as possible, fit for combat, but there are also medical grounds for this kind of treatment.

149

The swelling around the injured joint is due to fluid secreted in the tissue: if this is allowed to remain at rest, fibrous strands and accretions will be formed, and recovery takes longer. If a sprained ankle is not exercised, the patient is liable to suffer pain for a long time. When the joint is manipulated a crackling sound can be heard as all the accretions break, and the patient can immediately be relieved of pain.

Something similar applies in the case of many back complaints, where several joints are affected and produce accretions; then can be cured by special manipulation, the best possible effect being achieved with an anaesthetic of short duration, when the muscles are relaxed, the joints are allowed more mobility and crackling is liable to be particularly prominent.

This is the customary treatment at orthopaedic hospitals in Great Britain, and one which I became more familiar with after the war, when I worked there for a few years. I have since turned this treatment to good account in my practice as an orthopaedic surgeon, but it is important to consider critically what kind of dorsal complaint one manipulates, as there are some that should not be treated in this way.

This effective treatment resulted in a greater turnover of patients in our ward, which made it easier to satisfy the need for hospital beds.

In the surgical ward, to which I was later posted, wounds and fractures were treated; our problems were much the same as at the base hospital in Finland in 1940. But there was one innovation: penicillin had arrived. It was more effective than the sulfa drugs previously in use. After wounds had been cleaned they could now be sewn up straight away. In the case of open fractures, too, the wound could be stitched together as soon as the fracture had been operated and placed in position prior to being put in plaster. Penicillin was especially useful in dealing with the nasty wounds and fractures caused by exploding land-mines. These necessitate major operations, occasionally amputation and protracted treatment.

However, there were quite a number of cases of wounds infected with gas gangrene, which is a very serious condition. While the penicillin deals effectively with the germ, the gas forming around it prevents the penicillin from penetrating. Patients in this condition were often in a very bad way, and in many cases died.

As our base hospital belonged to the 21st Army Group, and served the needs of both British and Canadian troops, our medical staff had been recruited from both countries, and the chief surgeon in our ward was a Canadian major. The hospital had many wards, and a large medical staff, and many nurses and assistants.

Just outside the gate one could catch a tram to the centre of Brussels, a highly interesting city thronged with motley crowds, and with many service people, on short leave from the front, enjoying a leisurely stroll in the streets. The main square was dominated by beautiful old buildings on all sides, and everyone was keen to see the celebrated Mannikin Pis statue with its little fountain. V1 bombs en route for England would often whizz by overhead. These could be seen approaching horizontally, and as soon as the engine cut out it was possible to gauge more or less where they would drop, and take all possible precautions. By contrast the V2 would plummet to earth without prior warning, and if one were close enough an extra bang could be heard due to the supersonic speed with which it was falling.

When peace was concluded on 7th May there was great rejoicing in town. That evening the streets all of a sudden were lit up, and thronged with people in festive spirit. It was as though the sun had started to shine again.

I stayed on at the hospital for another week, and on 14th May I returned to London, crossing the Channel by boat and continuing by train.

I returned to a city that was different: there were admittedly bomb sites and ruined buildings, but people were smiling and laughing, and the street lights betokened that now at last the war was over. I celebrated Norway's National Day, 17th May, in the company of my countrymen, happy at our regained freedom. Though we were in a foreign land, and there were no birch trees, the brightly lit streets at night made it a red-letter day.

About a week later I travelled to Scotland, and at Leith a large passenger liner, the "Baufora," was full to the gunwhales with eager Norwegians.

The sight of the Norwegian coast was a joyous encounter. After a stop-off in Stavanger we continued along the coast, past familiar landmarks to Oslo, where we docked on Friday, 1st June.

To Murmansk with Russian Prisoners of War

At the beginning of July, after a short spell of work in the DMS's office in Oslo, I was ordered north: I was to assist in the evacuation of Russian prisoners of war from Rana to Murmansk. I took the train to Trondheim, and from there the coastal steamer to Tromsø, calling on the way at Narvik on 9th July, when there was a total eclipse of the sun.

In Tromsø I boarded the Kong Haakon VII, a Liberty ship, one of a type which had been mass-produced in the U.S.A. since 1942. These freighters were built at government expense on lines devised by Henry J. Kaiser, whereby pre-fabricated hull sections were produced in various factories and welded together on the stocks. They were of 10,500 tons dwt, and 2,700 were built during the war, mainly to replace all the ships sunk in convoy across the Atlantic. A special feature of these ships was that they were launched sideways. They had a speed of only ten knots.

From Tromsø we made our way down to the POW camp at Mo in Rana, where Professor Leiv Kreyberg had been busy de-lousing the inmates and we continued with this prior to the prisoners embarking. The ship had been specially adapted for this kind of transport, with an extra covered deck. We embarked 1900 persons.

One of them had contracted pleurisy, and was very poorly, but there were no other serious cases of illness on board.

The ship's captain was called Jensen, but command was in the hands of British officers.

The voyage to Murmansk proved an interesting experience, as this was the route the convoys had taken.

The POWs were clearly delighted at the sight of their native land: they could hardly wait to land, and started to decorate the ship with flags, birch branches that they had brought along, and anything handy. Expectation mounted visibly as we approached the quay in Murmansk.

We were not exactly accorded the red carpet treatment: as soon as we were alongside Russian officers leapt on board, and ordered all POWs to parade on deck. They then strode down the line, stripping off all badges of rank. Smiles froze on the faces of the POWs, and an ominous silence prevailed, as they now realised the fate that awaited them. They could hardly have known that this would be a fate they would share with countless countrymen in the same situation.

They were prisoners once again, but now in their own country; they were ordered ashore, and marched off. I had a last glimpse of the pleurisy patient on a stretcher at the top of an overloaded truck disappearing behind a shed.

On the quay a number of women were busy unloading wood from a small freighter, apparently indifferent to what was going on. They were probably used to seeing shiploads of prisoners returning home, and knew what they are in for.

As we sailed away down the fjord I had an uncanny feeling that we were still not at peace.

The POWs we had with us were apparently rejoicing at the prospect of returning home; but of the over 80,000 who were in Norway, many were sent back much against their will and tried in various ways to avoid repatriation, fearing the worst. It was a sad epilogue to peace.

On my return to Oslo I continued for a while working at the DMS's office. In the autumn of 1945 I went back to Aker Hospital and resumed work in the post I had resigned from four years before.

Selected Sources

Riksarkivet, Oslo.

Public Records, Kew, London.

Naval Historical Library, London.

Scots Polar Research Institute, Cambridge.

Royal Geographical Society, London.

Öystein Fjærli: "Krigens Svalbard", Oslo.

J. D. M. Blyth: "German meteorological activities in Arctis 1940–45". Polar Record, Vol. 6, 1951.

Allied Convoys to Murmansk and Arkangelsk 1941–45. Polar Record, Vol. 5, 1950.

David Howarth: "Sledge Patrol".

Douglas Liversidge: "The Third Front". (Souvenir Press, London).

Clayton Knight—Robert Durham: "Hitch your wagon".

Ernst Ullring: "På langtur på Svalbard under krigen", Polarboken 1949.

W. Schwerdtfeger—F. Selinger: "Wetterflieger in der Arktis". Motorbuch Verlag, Stuttgart.

John Winton: "Carrier Glorious". Leo Cooper, London.

G. H. Liljequist: "Did the 'Josehine Ford" reach the North Pole?" Interavia no. 51/1960.

John Prebble: "Mutiny".

Sir Philip Joubert—A. R. Glen: High Latitude Flying By Coastal Command In Support of Convoys to North Russia. The Geographical Journal 108, 1946.

Martin Conway: No Man's Land.

Author's diaries.